Israel Pocket Library

IMMIGRATION and SETTLEMENT

KETER BOOKS

This book is compiled from material originally published in the *Encyclopaedia Judaica*

P.O.Box 7145, Jerusalem, Israel

Cat. No. 25065

ISBN 0 7065 1324 x

Printed in Israel

CONTENTS

1 INTRODUCTION 1

2 SECOND TEMPLE TO ḤIBBAT ZION 4
Itzhak Alfassi

3 ALIYAH (1880 – 1939) 13
Misha Louvish

4 "ILLEGAL" IMMIGRATION AND THE BERIḤAH 35
Yehuda Slutsky and Yehuda Bauer

5 STATE OF ISRAEL (1948 – 72) 50
Zvi Zinger (Yaron)

6 LAW OF RETURN 75
Meir Silverstone

7 YOUTH ALIYAH 79
Chanoch Rinott

8 SETTLEMENT 87
Dr. Raanan Weitz

9 LAND OWNERSHIP 103
Joseph Weitz

10 LAND RECLAMATION 109
Joseph Weitz

11 THE JEWISH NATIONAL FUND 112
Jacob Tsur

12 PLANNING AND DEVELOPMENT 117
Jacob Dash

13 HOUSING 122
David Tanne

GLOSSARY 133

ABBREVIATIONS 138

BIBLIOGRAPHY 140

INDEX 142

CONTRIBUTORS

Itzhak Alfassi; General Secretary, B'nai B'rith, Tel Aviv

Misha Louvish; Writer and journalist, Jerusalem

Yehuda Slutsky; Professor of History of the Israel Labor Movement, Tel Aviv University

Yehuda Bauer; Professor of Contemporary Jewry, Hebrew University of Jerusalem

Zvi Zinger (Yaron); The Jewish Agency, Jerusalem

Chanoch Rinott; Senior Teacher and Director of the Center for Jewish Education in the Diaspora, the Hebrew University of Jerusalem; former Director General of the Israel Ministry of Education

Meir Silverstone; Attorney and former Director General, Ministry of the Interior, Jerusalem

Dr. Raanan Weitz; Member of the World Zionist Executive; Director of the Settlement Study Center, Rehovot

Joseph Weitz (the late); Writer and former Head of the Development Authority of Jewish National Fund, Jerusalem

Jacob Dash; Head of the Planning Department, Ministry of the Interior, Jerusalem

Jacob Tsur; Former Ambassador of Israel in Latin America and France; Chairman of the Board of Directors, the Jewish National Fund, Jerusalem

David Tanne (the late); Chairman of the Board of Directors, Tefahot-Mortgage Bank; Former Director of the Ministry of Housing

1 INTRODUCTION

Aliyah, which means "ascension" or "going up," is the coming of Jews as individuals or in groups, from exile or diaspora to live in the Land of Israel. Those who "go up" for this purpose are known as *olim*—a term used in the Bible for the children of Israel who went up from Egypt (Gen. 50:14 and Num. 32:11) and, at a later period, for the exiles who returned from captivity in Babylon (Ezra 2:1, 59 and Neh. 5-6). The call of Cyrus—"Whosoever there is among you of all His people—his God be with him—let him go up . . ." (Ezra 1:3; II Chron. 36:23)—has been used as a watchword for *aliyah*. It was *aliyah* that re-created the Jewish commonwealth in the Land after the Babylonian Exile, provided the community with some of its prominent spiritual leaders during the Second Temple and subsequent periods, preserved and repeatedly renewed the Jewish presence in Ereẓ Israel during the periods of Byzantine, Arab, Mamluk, and Ottoman rule, and reestablished the State of Israel in modern times.

The following were the principal motives that led individuals and groups to leave the Diaspora to settle in Ereẓ Israel at various periods:

1) The divine commandment *(mitzvah)* to go to Ereẓ Israel and settle there. There is a dispute about this precept in the Talmud (Ket. 110–111a), where both advocates and opponents of *aliyah* are presented. The Tosafists stated that the precept was no longer in force, and Maimonides[1] did not include it in his list of *mitzvot*. Nahmanides[2] was the first to maintain that settlement in Ereẓ Israel was a

[1] Medieval Jewish authority and scholar; born in Spain, died in Egypt, 1204
[2] Medieval Jewish authority and scholar; born in Spain, died in Acre, 1270

commandment fixed for posterity. This assertion aroused controversy throughout halakhic literature. The dispute was revived with the appearance of the Ḥovevei Zion who advanced the commandment to go to Ereẓ Israel, in addition to national and social factors, as a reason for settlement. In the heat of the argument a new position was formulated by some of the orthodox, who argued that not only is it not a *mitzvah* to go to Ereẓ Israel but it is even forbidden, as it contradicts the oath sworn by the Jews: "That Israel shall not go up [all together as if surrounded] by a wall," and that "they shall not rebel against the nations of the world" (Ket. 111a).

2) The desire to study the Torah in Ereẓ Israel, where the Sanhedrin and the great academies were to be found. *Aliyah* for this purpose occurred mainly in the tannaitic and part of the amoraic periods, and has recurred in modern times with the increase in the number of important yeshivot in Ereẓ Israel. There have been cases of entire yeshivot moving to Israel.

3) The belief that one who is buried in Ereẓ Israel has many privileges (TJ, Kil. 9:4, 32c; Gen. R. 96), which led many elderly people to come to Ereẓ Israel in order to die there. This belief existed during the time of the Temple, although it was attacked by some of the talmudic sages (Gen. R. 96:5). Characteristic of this outlook in later generations were the statements of Solomon Shlomel, a disciple of the 16th-century mystic Isaac Luria ("He who was privileged by God to fix his home in Ereẓ Israel is blessed, and blessed is he who can attain the World to Come").

4) The belief that only in Ereẓ Israel can one fulfill the *mitzvot* of the Torah. This was the watchword of the Karaites in the ninth to 11th centuries, and was stressed by religious groups during the period of the Ḥovevei Zion.

5) The persecution of the Jews in Europe. Beginning with the 13th century, Jewish refugees, in order to escape persecution in Europe, began to go to Ereẓ Israel since it was not under Christian rule. There are several questions in the
 halakhah concerning those who vowed in times of stress to

emigrate to Ereẓ Israel and broke their vows when the trouble had passed.

6) The messianic factor and the anticipation of redemption. Emigration to Ereẓ Israel would help to bring the advent of the Messiah nearer. The following statement of Raphael Mordecai Malki (late 17th century) is characteristic of this approach: "It is a known fact that the Messiah son of Ephraim does not come and is not revealed before 100 or 200 people (as in Jerusalem today), but before thousands and tens of thousands." The emigration of kabbalists after the expulsion from Spain in 1492 was considered to be due to messianic motivations—a letter dated 1521 announces that signs of the redemption are at hand. So are the *aliyyot* of the disciples of Elijah the Gaon of Vilna[3] and the Ḥasidim, though the messianic factor in the ḥasidic *aliyah* is a subject of dispute among contemporary historians, some of whom think that it was motivated by the desire to win Ereẓ Israel for Ḥasidism.

7) The curing of illness and barrenness.

8) National and social factors.

There were many difficulties standing in the way of those coming to Ereẓ Israel. Transportation was arduous and irregular. Many of the ships which set sail for Ereẓ Israel were dilapidated and they sometimes sank with all their passengers. Menahem Mendel of Vitebsk, leader of the ḥasidic *aliyah* of 1777, boasts that only one ship sank on his voyage. In addition there were cruel captains and pirates, who sometimes murdered their passengers or sold them into slavery. Large ransoms often had to be paid by various Jewish communities. As a result of these difficulties, there arose the halakhic question of whether it was permissible, for reasons of safety, for a convoy to continue its journey through the desert on the Sabbath. In addition to the many difficulties encountered by travelers on arrival, there were the harsh political and economic conditions in Ereẓ Israel itself. Despite this, *aliyah* encompassed all currents of Judaism and all Diaspora communities.

[3] Talmudic authority; died in Vilna, 1797

2 SECOND TEMPLE TO ḤIBBAT ZION

During the time of the Second Temple there were many immigrants to Ereẓ Israel. A famous example is the *aliyah* of Hillel, who went from Babylonia poor and without means, and later became the head of the Sanhedrin, founding a long line of *nesi'im* (leaders). One of the high priests appointed by Herod was Hananel ha-Bavli, i.e., of Babylonia. *Aliyah,* mainly from Babylonia, did not cease after the destruction of the Second Temple (70 C.E.). Sources cite many immigrant scholars who achieved a prominent place in the Jewish community of Ereẓ Israel. In the third generation of *tannaim* after the destruction of the Temple (110–135 C.E.), Hanan ha-Miẓri ("of Egypt"; Yoma 63b) and Yose b. Dormaskos, who went from Damascus (Sif. Deut. 1), are mentioned. The next generation (135–170 C.E.) included R. Johanan ha-Sandelar of Alexandria (TJ, Hag. 3:1, 78d) and R. Nathan ha-Bavli, who was the son of the exilarch in Babylonia. Among the fifth generation of *tannaim* are (170–200) R. Ḥiyya the Great, the disciple and colleague of Judah ha-Nasi (Er. 73a), and Issi b. Judah (Pes. 113b), both of whom emigrated from Babylonia, and Menahem the Gaul (i.e., France; TJ, Ber. 4:4, 8b).

Aliyah from Babylonia did not cease in the amoraic period, despite the fact that the great centers of Jewish scholarship were located there. Of the first generation of *amoraim* (220–250) R. Ḥanina b. Ḥama, a disciple of Judah ha-Nasi and one of the greatest *amoraim* in Ereẓ Israel, emigrated from Babylonia (TJ, Pe'ah 7:4, 20a). In the second generation (250–290), Eleazar b. Pedat, *rosh yeshivah* in Tiberias (Ḥul. 111b), R. Zakkai (TJ, Shab. 7:1,

9a) and R. Ḥiyya b. Joseph (Ḥul. 54a), who emigrated from Babylonia, and Ḥinena Kartigna'ah (of Carthage; TJ, Shab. 16:2, 15c) are mentioned. The latter attests emigration from Africa. Two *amoraim* called Rav Kahana also emigrated from Babylonia (Zev. 59a). There was a particularly large *aliyah* among the third and fourth generations of *amoraim* (290–320), some of the immigrants forming the leadership of the Jewish community in Ereẓ Israel.

The proclamation by the Roman emperor Constantine I (the Great) of Christianity as the official religion of the state in 323 and his persecution of the Jews in his dominions initiated the decline of Jewry in Ereẓ Israel. In this period—the fifth generation of *amoraim,* in which the Jerusalem Talmud was completed—the stream of immigrants from Babylonia stopped almost completely. The statements of the *amora* R. Abiathar (250–290 C.E.), who opposed the *aliyah* of Jews who left their families behind without a livelihood (Git. 6b), attest that the flow of *aliyah* was coming to an end. In 520, Mar Zutra, a descendant of the exilarchs in Babylonia, settled in Tiberias and was appointed head of the academy. Because the times were not conducive to *aliyah,* only individuals came.

There is little information on *aliyah* in the next few centuries, in which the Muslim conquest took place (636–38), but the *aliyah* of R. Aḥa of Shabḥa, one of the greatest Babylonian scholars, who came in about 750, is well known and other disciples probably immigrated with him. The Karaites, who proclaimed to their faithful: "Be assembled in the holy city and gather your brethren," began their *aliyah* as early as the ninth century. Among them was the author Daniel b. Moses al-Qūmisi. A Karaite legend attributes the beginnings of their community in Ereẓ Israel to the founder of the sect, Anan b. David. In the tenth century a cultural efflorescence took place among the Karaites in Ereẓ Israel, among whom were Sahl b. Maẓli'aḥ and Salmon b. Jeroḥam, and the Karaite community spread to Ramleh. In the 11th century important arrivals included Solomon b. Judah, from Morocco, head of the Academy in Jerusalem and Ramleh (1025–1051), and the *nasi* Daniel b. Azariah, a scion of the exilarchs of Babylonia. From the 12th century, testimonies of travelers and not of immigrants have been preserved; the political situation under the Crusaders did not facilitate *aliyah.* According to a famous legend (now known to be untrue) Judah Halevi[4] went to Ereẓ Israel in 1141 and was killed at the gates of Jerusalem. In 1165 Maimon b. Joseph, the father of Maimonides, went there with his sons, but left after six months. In the late 12th century more Jews from North Africa arrived as a result of the persecutions there during the Almohad regime. Benjamin of Tudela found approximately 1,000 Jewish families during his stay in Ereẓ Israel (c. 1170). Ten years later, Pethahiah of Regensburg[5] mentioned a much smaller number. According to Judah Al-Ḥarizi [6], who traveled to Ereẓ Israel in 1218, Saladin invited the Jews to settle in the land in 1190, after his victory over the Crusaders. Al-Ḥarizi stated: "From the time when the Ishmaelites [Arabs] occupied the land, Jews settled there" (*Taḥkemoni,* ed. A. Kaminka (1899), No. 28, p. 245).

Persecution of Jews in Europe also contributed to *aliyah.* The most important immigration of this wave was that of the "300 French and English rabbis" who went to Ereẓ Israel in 1210–11. According to an anonymous source: "The king honored them greatly and built synagogues and academies there . . . A miracle occurred when they prayed for rain and were answered, and thus they sanctified God's name" (*Shevet Yehudah,* ed. Azriel Shochat (1947), 147). There are many opinions as to the causes of this *aliyah.* Horodezky[7] holds that it resulted from spiritual pressure—the decline in Torah study in France; in contrast, Dubnow[8] believes that it stemmed from severe economic oppression (*Divrei Yemei Am Olam,* pt. 5, p. 15). A new and improbable view has been advanced: that the purpose was

[4] Leading medieval Spanish Hebrew poet, died in Egypt, 1141

[5] 12th-century traveler

[6] Spanish Hebrew poet and translator, died c. 1235

[7] Scholar of Ḥasidism, died in Israel, 1957

[8] Jewish historian; killed in Riga ghetto, 1941

to establish a Sanhedrin—in accordance with Maimonides' opinion that the establishment of a Sanhedrin is a condition for redemption. In about 1260, there were more *olim* from these countries, including Jehiel b. Joseph of Paris, whose yeshivah in Acre was called by the name of his town, Midrash ha-Gadol de-Parisi. The most important *aliyah* in this century was that of Naḥmanides in 1267. Since his arrival, settlement is said to have been continuous in Jerusalem; hence his title "*Avi ha-Yishuv*" ("Father of the Community"). In the late 13th century, *aliyah* ceased as a result of the fierce battles between the Crusaders and the Muslims. The expulsion from France (1306) led R. Estori ha-Parḥi, the first Jew to write a geography of Ereẓ Israel, to come to the Land in about 1322. Many came from Spain and Germany in the 14th century, as stated in a letter from a disciple of Naḥmanides: "At present many have arisen willingly to emigrate to Ereẓ Israel." Among those who came from Spain was the kabbalist Rabbi Shem Tov b. Abraham Gaon, who wrote his *Keter Shem Tov* in Ereẓ Israel. In the 15th century Jewish pilgrims and prospective *olim* had to fight against a new obstacle: an order by Pope Martin V (1428) forbidding Italian ships to transport Jews to Ereẓ Israel. This decree remained in force for only a very brief period but it was renewed toward the end of the century, and led to many wanderings in order to circumvent the sea routes, if possible—for instance, as suggested by R. Isaac Ẓarefati in a letter to the Jews, via Turkey. A number of Italian Jews went to Ereẓ Israel in the 15th century and made their mark on the Jewish community. Among them were Elijah of Ferrara, who wrote a letter of great importance for the history of *aliyah* in the late 14th and early 15th centuries, and members of his family. The Ashkenazi Joseph da Montagna came from Italy via Venice and was appointed *dayyan* in Jerusalem at the end of 1481. Isaac b. Meir Latif apparently came from Ancona in about 1480.

Immigrants from Mesopotamia, Persia, India, China, Yemen, and North Africa are also mentioned in this century. Yemenite Jews came in caravans from Aden and Turkey, e.g., R. Abraham b. Solomon Treves of Constantinople. The increase in *aliyah* between 1488 and 1495 is attested by the fact that in 1495 it was difficult to find a place to live in Jerusalem. The most important of the Italian scholars who immigrated to Ereẓ Israel was R. Obadiah of Bertinoro, who arrived in 1488 after three years of wandering. In his letters he writes about other *aliyyot* from Italy and under his influence the number of immigrants increased. In a letter written in 1495, an anonymous student of his praises his master's manifold activities in Jerusalem and he tells of immigrants from Italy and Sicily, some of whom had drowned. After the Turkish conquest (1516), many Jews from the Orient, Sicily, Italy, France, and Germany, as well as refugees from the Spanish and Portuguese expulsions, immigrated to Ereẓ Israel. One of them was R. Isaac Sholal ha-Kohen, the last *nagid* of Egypt, whose *aliyah* (1517) was of great importance in the development of the Jewish community in Jerusalem. The immigration of Spanish Jews with their characteristic laws, manners, language, and customs had an important impact on the community. Some of them settled in Jerusalem—the most important being the kabbalist Abraham b. Eliezer ha-Levi and Levi Ibn Ḥabib—but most of them settled in Safed, notably Joseph Saracosti, Jacob Berab, Joseph Caro, Moses Cordovero, Moses Galante, and David b. Abi Zimra. The immigrants to Safed also included a considerable number from Italy, who even established an independent "Italian community." The extent of the increase of *aliyah* to Safed is attested by the fact that its population numbered 10,000 in the mid-16th century, while according to the Yemenite traveler Zechariah al-Ḍāhiri, it numbered 14,000 in 1567. A great role in *aliyah* was played by the immigrants from North Africa.

The flourishing of the Kabbalah in Safed contributed to additional *aliyah*, which continued throughout the 16th century, from France, Germany, Italy, and other European countries, as well as from North Africa and the Orient.

Ofen (Buda) served as a gathering place for Jews from France and Germany, who could travel from there in convoy via Turkish territory. Important newcomers were R. Bezalel Ashkenazi, author of *Shitah Mekubbeẓet*, who arrived in 1588 and became head of the community in Jerusalem, and R. Isaiah ha Levi Horowitz (author of *Shenei Luḥot ha-Berit*), who came in 1621 and became head of the Ashkenazi community in Jerusalem, whose members were "multiplying greatly, literally by hundreds, and constructing great buildings" (letter to his sons). In the early 17th century a renewed *aliyah* of Karaites began, but the persecutions of Ibn Farukh (1625–27) slowed down the influx. Nevertheless, immigrants continued to arrive.

Shabbateanism (Shabbetai Ẓevi 1626–76) stimulated a new wave of longing for *aliyah*. Rumors of vast *aliyyot* spread everywhere; there were rumors of "80 ships" from Amsterdam and "400 families ready to depart" from Frankfort. However, this enthusiasm died out with the apostasy of Shabbetai Ẓevi. The only great *aliyah* that occurred as a result of Shabbateanism was that led by R. Judah Ḥasid and Ḥayyim Malakh (both crypto-Shabbateans) at the turn of the 17th century. There was no *aliyah* like it for many generations before or after it until modern times. In its beginnings the group numbered only 31 families, but more joined it along the way. The enormous influence of the emissaries of the immigrants, who assembled at Nikolsburg (Mikulov) for departure, is attested by an eyewitness, the German author J. J. Schudt (*Juedische Merckwuerdigkeiten*, 2 (Frankfort on the Main, 1714), 58). On its arrival the convoy numbered about 1,500—some said 1,700. There was a serious setback, however, when R. Judah Ḥasid died immediately after the group's arrival in Jerusalem and the lack of sources of livelihood, illness, and anti-Shabbatean persecutions contributed to the dispersal of the new arrivals. The *aliyah* of R. Abraham Rovigo from Modena, Italy, in 1702, with a convoy of 25 persons was also influenced by Shabbateanism.

But these were not the only convoys. According to one

emissary, the Jewish community in Jerusalem numbered 10,000 persons in 1741. Ḥayyim Abulafia came from Smyrna in 1740 and reestablished the yeshivah in Tiberias. Moses Ḥayyim Luzzatto[9] and his family arrived in 1743, although his activities in Ereẓ Israel were less important than his work in the Diaspora. There was an important *aliyah* of Turkish Jews at the time, including Gedaliah Ḥayyun, who founded Beth El, the *bet ha-midrash* of the kabbalists in Jerusalem, and the Rosanes, Gabbai, Naḥmias, and Pardo families. There were also Shalom Sharabi, a Yemenite immigrant, who held a position of prominence in Jerusalem, and Eleazer Rokeaḥ, the rabbi of Amsterdam, who settled in Safed. R. Ḥayyim b. Attar, author of *Or ha-Ḥayyim*, went from Salé (Morocco) in 1741 and established a yeshivah in Jerusalem. Nathan Bordjel, author of *Ḥok Nathan*, went from Tunis. An organized *aliyah* of proselytes, who settled in Safed and even sent a special emissary abroad, also took place in the 18th century.

The end of the 18th century marks the beginning of the *aliyah* of Ḥasidim, who made it a principle of their teachings. Ḥasidic legend describes at length how Israel Ba'al Shem Tov, the founder of Ḥasidism, longed to emigrate to Ereẓ Israel in order to meet with R. Ḥayyim b. Attar, and even made attempts to fulfill this wish, but was compelled to reconsider. His disciples, however, did everything to carry out their master's will. Thus, R. Abraham Gershon of Kutow (Kuty), the Ba'al Shem Tov's brother-in-law, emigrated with his family, and many Ḥasidim from Galicia and Volhynia followed him. The first organized *aliyah* of Ḥasidim took place in 1764, led by the Ba'al Shem Tov's disciples Menahem Mendel of Peremyshlyany, who settled in Jerusalem, and Naḥman of Horodenko in Tiberias. An *aliyah* of great value to the community in Ereẓ Israel took place in the spring (Adar) of 1777, 14 years after the first; it was led by Menahem Mendel of Vitebsk and Abraham of Kalisz, whose convoy numbered

[9] Italian Kabbalist and Hebrew poet: died of the plague in Acre, 1747

300 persons. They left Galatz, Rumania, in small boats for Constantinople and from there they sailed to Acre. The voyage lasted four months, and the convoy endured much hardship. They settled in Safed, where they met with many difficulties and most of them moved to Tiberias. This *aliyah* was rightly regarded as having revived Galilee and laid the basis for Jewish settlement in this region. More Ḥasidim came in subsequent generations, notably Abraham Dov of Ovruch in 1832, who headed the ḥasidic community of Safed, and Israel Bak, who brought his publishing house with him from Volhynia in 1831. The Ḥabad Ḥasidim formed another organized *aliyah,* consolidating the Ashkenazi community in Hebron, which was first organized by Ḥabad Ḥasidim from Safed and Tiberias. Ḥasidim have continued to come up to the present day.

At the same time the *Perushim,* the disciples of Elijah the Gaon of Vilna[10], also organized *aliyah,* establishing a community in Jerusalem. The Gaon of Vilna is reported to have made many efforts to go to Ereẓ Israel himself but did not meet with success. The first *Perushim* arrived as early as 1722, led by R. Israel of Shklov, but their impact was not noticeable and they did not even have a *minyan.* A second group, headed by Menahem Mendel of Shklov, arrived in 1808. Later, Saadiah b. Nathan Nata of Vilna and Nata b. Menahem Mendel of Shklov arrived. Menahem Mendel of Shklov and R. Israel of Shklov are rightly considered the fathers of their community in Jerusalem because of their initiative and powers of organization. Among other members of the community were Hillel Rivlin, scion of the prominent Rivlin family, R. Abraham Solomon Zalman Ẓoref; R. Shemariah Luria, a man of means who arrived with a convoy of 40 persons; R. Joseph Sundel of Salant, the spiritual father of the Musar movement[11]; and R. Samuel Salant, his son-in-law, who officiated as the city rabbi in Jerusalem for many years. It is of interest that these *aliyyot* included not only scholars but also artisans.

[10] See above
[11] Ethical movement originating in 19th-century Lithuania

In 1830 the *aliyah* from Germany began, led by Moses Sacks, the first who thought of large-scale productivization of the Jewish community in Ereẓ Israel. The German immigrants included Jehoseph Schwarz (arrived in 1833), the author of *Tevu'ot ha-Areẓ*, the most thorough work on Ereẓ Israel since the 14th-century *Kaftor va-Feraḥ*, and R. Eliezer Bergman. A notable *aliyah* came from Holland, which eventually merged with the German *aliyah* to form a joint community known as *Kolel 'HOD'* (Holland-Deutschland). There was also a sizable *aliyah* from Hungary, which was inspired by R. Moses Sofer, the author of *Ḥatam Sofer*, and played an important role in Jerusalem, though it consisted mostly of individuals, largely youths. Noteworthy are R. Israel Ze'ev Horowitz, Abraham Sha'ag, and Akiva Joseph Schlesinger. As they increased, they formed a separate *kolel*, as did the Polish immigrants. In the 19th century sizable *aliyyot* took place from the oriental countries as well, including Turkey, North Africa, Iraq, Persia, Bukhara, Kurdistan, Afghanistan, the Caucasus, and Yemen.

3 ALIYAH (1880–1939)

The First Aliyah. The beginnings of the modern Jewish return to the Land of Israel, which laid the foundations for the establishment of the State of Israel, were due to a combination of three causes: the age-old devotion of the Jews to their historic homeland and the hope of messianic redemption; the intensification of the intolerable conditions under which Jews lived in Eastern Europe; and the efforts of an active minority convinced that the return to the homeland was the only lasting and fundamental solution to the Jewish problem.

In the early 1880s the growing oppression of the Jews assumed acute forms in several Eastern European countries: the pogroms and repression that followed the assassination of Alexander II of Russia; the restriction of Jewish autonomy in Galicia; the pogroms and the restrictions imposed on Jewish trade in Rumania; and the Tisza-Eszlar blood libel in Hungary. A spontaneous mass migration movement was the result: between 1880 and 1900 over a million Jews fled from persecution and poverty to the United States. The hopes of the Haskalah movement for a normalization of the Jewish position through education and enlightenment had been shattered; the Jewish masses were on the move.

Simultaneously with this headlong flight to the New World, another Jewish migration movement, infinitesimally smaller but radically different in character, arose. A handful of young men felt that it was not enough to run away from persecution: the time had come to take the first step toward a fundamental solution of the Jewish problem: the return of the Jews to the Land of Israel. This vital first step must be to go up to live in the Promised Land and cultivate its soil. Branches of the new Ḥibbat Zion movement sprang up all over Eastern Europe, especially in Russia, though they had to meet in secret and their members ran a risk of arrest. The best-known section of the movement, Bilu, defined its aim as "the political, economic, and national-spiritual revival of the Jewish people in Syria and Ereẓ Israel." On July 7, 1882, a small group of 14—including one woman—landed at Jaffa and made its way to the Mikveh Israel training farm, founded in 1870, where it was given work. Further contingents followed, bringing the number of settlers up to over 50. The unaccustomed work was hard, the pay was wretched, and the novices were treated with contempt by the farm manager. Some of the Bilu'im moved to Jerusalem, where they formed a short-lived cooperative carpenters' workshop. Others received a plot to cultivate in Rishon le-Zion, but the crops were poor. Hopes that the Ḥibbat Zion movement abroad would help them buy land for a settlement of their own were disappointed, and the movement began to disintegrate. The Bilu'im were saved by Yehiel Pines, who bought 800 acres of land in the southern Shephelah, where they founded the village of Gederah, and appealed to Ḥibbat Zion abroad to defray the cost.

Meanwhile, Ḥibbat Zion had been organizing groups to settle in Ereẓ Israel. In January 1882, a conference at Focsani, Rumania, had decided to send out representatives to buy land, to be followed almost immediately by the first group of *olim* (sing. *oleh*), who would settle in the country. The Turkish government immediately ordered the cessation of Jewish immigration, and efforts to secure the withdrawal of the ban by appeals to Laurence Oliphant[12] and by representations at Constantinople were unsuccessful. The pioneers were undeterred, however; by 1884 six settlements had been established (including Gederah), and Petaḥ Tikvah revived. Four were supported by Baron Edmond de Rothschild[13], the other three being the responsibility of

[12] British non-Jewish proto-Zionist

[13] French philanthropist who supported Zionist settlement

Immigrants of the First Aliyah in front of their tents, c. 1900. Courtesy Central Zionist Archives, Jerusalem.

Ḥibbat Zion. In the same year the first international conference of Ḥibbat Zion, with 35 delegates from Russia, Rumania, Germany, Britain, and France, met at Katowice and established a provisional central committee in Odessa. The number of societies reached close to 100, with 14,000 members who collected about 30,000 rubles a year, as well as 20,000 rubles from various campaigns. Ramified propaganda was carried out in many parts of Europe and in America.

In these early beginnings, many of the characteristic features of modern *aliyah* were already present in embryo. Like the later Zionist movement, Ḥibbat Zion consisted of three main strata: a large periphery of uncommitted sympathizers; smaller groups of organized members, who propagated the idea and collected funds for practical work; and a still smaller nucleus, without whom nothing could have been done, who followed the principle of *hagshamah aẓmit* ("personal implementation"), to use another term that was current at later stages. Some of those who contributed to the cost of the work did so out of belief in the aims of the movement; others, as in later years, were moved by purely philanthropic motives, or a mixture of the two. There were also rudimentary arrangements in the country to help the newcomers: the Mikveh Israel farm helped to train them; local Jewish leaders cooperated with Ḥibbat Zion missions; Baron de Rothschild sent out officials to administer his benefactions; in 1891 an abortive attempt was made to set up an executive of Ḥibbat Zion in Jaffa, headed by Vladimir Tiomkin.

Although the seeds of later developments were there, their growth at first was painfully slow. The entire effort would have collapsed but for the benevolence of Rothschild, whose money not only bought land and implements, built homes, and purchased the crops, but also erected synagogues and schools, hospitals and old-age asylums. His administrators, many of whom were corrupt, kept the settlers on a tight rein, however, and stifled any signs of independence. The advent of Theodor Herzl and the founding of the World Zionist Organization in 1897, while arousing a tidal wave of enthusiasm in the Jewish world, had little effect at the time in the Land of Israel itself, as the new movement devoted most of its energies to political work in the hope of obtaining a charter for the establishment of a Jewish autonomous territory. The idealism of the settlers was withering away under the pressure of the difficult conditions; most of the new villages employed cheap Arab labor, and the enterprise, started with such high hopes, was producing not a self-reliant community of cheap cultivators, but a class of colonists, with the shallowest of roots in the soil, which was still—even when owned by Jews—being tilled mainly by the native Arab population.

By 1903, the end of the First Aliyah period, a score of new villages had been founded, 350,000 dunams (almost 90,000 acres) of land had been purchased, and some 10,000 Jews had settled in the country, over half of them on the soil. There were also beginnings of urban settlement, especially in Jaffa, where 3,000 newcomers had made their homes. Hebrew was beginning to be a spoken tongue once again, and the first Hebrew elementary schools had been established, though French culture, propagated by the Alliance Israélite Universelle[14] and the Rothschild administration, was widespread. On the whole, however, the pioneering drive had been exhausted and a period of stagnation had set in.

The Second Aliyah. The depression caused by the stagnation of the first settlements, the controversies in the Zionist Organization over the Uganda Scheme, and the death of Herzl in 1904 were followed by a new upsurge of pioneering fervor which produced the Second Aliyah. The first impetus of the new wave came from the Kishinev pogroms of 1903 and the others that followed two years later. The impotence of the great Russian community in the face of these savage mob attacks shocked thousands of young Jews into a new determination to build a Jewish homeland. Many of them were imbued with socialist ideals and, sorely disappointed by the failure of the 1905 Revolution, decided that they must create their own revolutionary movement on the basis of national revival.

These young men and women were guided not only by a more conscious and consistent national ideology, but also by the ideal of laying the foundations for a workers' commonwealth in the Land of Israel. Naḥman Syrkin had already advocated an organic synthesis of Zionism and Socialism. The Socialist-Zionist philosophy of the Po'alei Zion movement, formulated by Ber Borochov, was founded on a Marxist analysis of the Jewish problem that led to the conclusion that social and economic forces were working for the Socialist-Zionist solution. Others, under the influence of A. D. Gordon's philosophy of labor, founded the Ha-Po'el ha-Ẓa'ir movement, which emphasized the importance of physical labor, rather than the socialist reorganization of society, as the foundation of national

[14]French Jewish organization to help Jews in other countries.

Loading wheat at the threshing floor, Gederah, 1913.
Courtesy Central Zionist Archives, Jerusalem.

revival. Both parties added to the idea of personal participation in the building of the homeland the concept of *avodah aẓmit* ("personal labor").

Among the youth organizations set up at this time was one called He-Ḥalutz ("The Pioneer") in Rumania—the first to use the name. Unlike their elders, its members were not content to make propaganda, collect funds, and prepare for an undefined future. They organized only to make preparations for the journey; once a group, usually consisting of young people from the same town, had gone out, it would make way for another, which would go through the same process. In 1905 a He-Ḥalutz society was set up in the United States, and in 1911 Joseph Trumpeldor tried to establish a countrywide organization in Russia with a detailed plan for organized training in the Diaspora and activity in the Land of Israel, but the project was dropped when he himself left Russia to settle in Ereẓ Israel.

The pioneers of the Second Aliyah were also much more self-reliant than their predecessors. As there was no possibility of exercising political influence on the government of the country, the parties engaged in practical work, looking after the housing, employment, and, later, the health and welfare of the newcomers. The Zionist Organization had also started practical work in the Land of Israel. The Jewish National Fund was founded in 1901, and two years later the Anglo-Palestine Company (later the Anglo-Palestine Bank) was established in Jaffa as a subsidiary of the Jewish Colonial Trust; in 1908 Arthur Ruppin set up the Palestine Office in Jaffa. The workers, however, were far from passive. In 1907 Joseph Vitkin issued a call for more pioneers, which, coming from one of those who had led the way, had greater force than the exhortations of Zionist leaders in the Diaspora. The workers fought not only for better conditions, but also for the right to employment on the Jewish farms, and in 1909 it was their initiative that led to the establishment of the first kevuẓah, the harbinger of a new type of social unit. They were also active in the beginnings of Jewish self-defense (Ha-Shomer) and the introduction of Hebrew into all spheres of life. By

Mounted guards of Ha-Shomer in Galilee, c. 1910.
Courtesy Haganah Historical Archives, Tel Aviv.

the beginning of World War I the *yishuv,* 85,000 strong, was a source of inspiration to the movement abroad and a magnet for further *aliyah.*

The Development of He-Ḥalutz. The Third Aliyah, which started in 1919, was partially a continuation of the second, which had been interrupted by the war. A renewed impetus, the result of the Bolshevik Revolution and the postwar pogroms and excesses in the Ukraine, Poland, and Hungary, coincided with a renewed hope, inspired by the Balfour Declaration and the British conquest of Palestine. The westward road to the United States was still open, and most of those who chose the Land of Israel did so out of Zionist convictions. In 1915–16 David Ben-Gurion and Izhak Ben-Zvi, exiled from the Land of Israel by the Turks, had founded a He-Ḥalutz organization in the United States, which merged with the movement for joining the Jewish Legion. A larger and more lasting pioneering organization arose in Russia after the February Revolution of 1917. A national council of He-Ḥalutz groups in Russia

Unit of the **Jewish Legion** at El-Arish, 1918. Courtesy Central Zionist Archives, Jerusalem.

met in January 1918, and the first conference of the Russian He-Ḥalutz movement took place a year later in Moscow under Trumpeldor's leadership. He-Ḥalutz gave the underlying principles of the previous *aliyah* movements a more definite and consistent form. Its members belonged to the World Zionist Organization, accepted its authority, and took part in its activities, especially the work of the Jewish National Fund. It was not a party body, though it regarded itself as a part of the Jewish labor movement, and its members in the Land of Israel helped to forge the degree of labor unity which led to the establishment of the Histadrut.

He-Ḥalutz set up a network of training centers in the Diaspora in which its members studied the ideals of the movement, learned Hebrew and its literature, and gained experience in manual labor and farming. Some groups found employment with non-Jewish farmers; others set up their own training farms. To some extent, this stage was regarded as a regrettable necessity in the absence of immediate facilities for *aliyah*, but it ensured that the young men and women arrived not as complete novices, but equipped with a consistent social philosophy, some experience of living in communes, and at least some rudimentary skills. Even while in the Diaspora, they submitted themselves to the democratic discipline of the movement and were ready to set out for the Land of Israel whenever called upon to do so. Contact was maintained with those who had gone on ahead through emissaries *(sheliḥim)* from Palestine who knew the conditions and spent several months or years in the Diaspora as instructors and leaders. The training farms and communes also performed a valuable function as centers of attraction for youth, who could thus see the principles of the movement put into practice even in the Diaspora.

There were also two other main pioneering organizations: Betar, affiliated to the Revisionist organization, and He-Ḥalutz ha-Mizrachi. A non-party religious pioneering body, Baḥad (Berit Ḥalutzim Datiyyim—"League of Religious Pioneers"), was founded in Germany and later spread to Britain and other countries.

The Zionist Movement and Aliyah. When the Zionist movement started to rebuild its organization immediately after World War I, *aliyah* and settlement were, of course, among its major concerns. The Central Office established in London had sections for immigration and agricultural settlement. The 1920 London Conference, held instead of a regular Zionist Congress, decided that the Jewish National Fund should safeguard Jewish labor on its land and assist the settlement of Jewish agricultural workers on their own farms. A Central Immigration Office was to be opened in Palestine without delay, with Palestine Offices in all countries from which *ḥalutzim* might come. Each office was to be controlled by a committee representing the local Zionist parties in proportion to their size. They were to give preference to candidates for *aliyah* who had been trained as farm workers or artisans, could speak Hebrew, and were physically fit.

The contributions of Diaspora Jewry to the cost of immigration and settlement were to be channeled through a new agency, Keren Hayesod, the Foundation Fund, which was to be an instrument of voluntary self-taxation on the principle of the biblical tithe (though this quota was not actually reached in practice). The 12th Zionist Congress in 1921 resolved that Palestine Offices should be set up in the chief ports of embarkation —Trieste in Italy and Constanta in Rumania—as well as the principal lands of emigration, and undertook to subsidize the vocational training of the *ḥalutzim.* Of the executive of 13, six members were to sit in Jerusalem and take charge of affairs in Palestine. Thus the World Zionist Organization, with its democratically elected and controlled legislative and executive organs, representing Jews throughout the world who were devoted to the idea of national revival, established the machinery for financing, fostering, and controlling *aliyah* and settlement as the basic methods for establishing the Jewish National Home.

 Aliyah, however, was now also a major issue in the

relations between the Zionist movement and the non-Jewish population of Palestine, in the policy of the British government and its administration in the country, and, through the League of Nations Mandate, in international affairs. Although Winston Churchill as colonial secretary rejected Arab demands in 1920 for the stoppage of Jewish immigration, *aliyah* was in fact suspended temporarily after Arab attacks on Jews in 1921. The Churchill White Paper of 1922, while affirming that Jewish immigrants must continue, stated that it "cannot be so great in volume as to exceed whatever may be the economic capacity of the country at the time to absorb new arrivals" and that "the immigrants should not be a burden upon the people of Palestine as a whole."

The Mandatory Power and Aliyah. The Mandate for Palestine recognized the Zionist Organization's right to advise and cooperate with the administration in matters affecting the establishment of the Jewish National Home and the interests of the Jewish population and instructed the administration to "facilitate Jewish immigration under suitable conditions and . . . encourage . . . close settlement by Jews on the Land," adding the limitation: "while ensuring that the rights and position of other sections of the population are not prejudiced." This reservation, as well as the phrase "under suitable conditions," was frequently cited in later years by the British as justification for severe restrictions on Jewish immigration, which hampered the development of the Jewish National Home. Arab pressure for the stoppage of *aliyah,* reinforced by repeated and violent attacks on the Jews and the restrictions imposed by the British in response to this pressure from time to time, constituted a leading, perhaps the major, theme in the political history of Palestine throughout the Mandatory period.

In September 1920, shortly after the establishment of the British Civil Administration in Palestine, an Immigration Ordinance was issued authorizing the Zionist Organization to bring in 16,500 immigrants per annum, provided that it

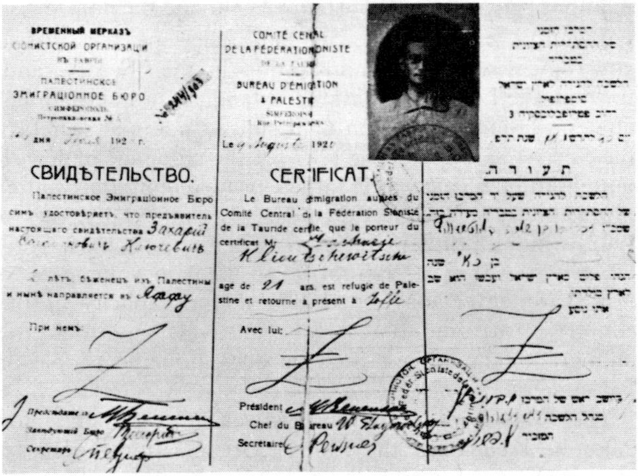
ВРЕМЕННЫЙ МЕРКАЗЪ
СІОНИСТСКОЙ ОРГАНИЗАЦИИ
ПАЛЕСТИНСКОЕ
ЭМИГРАЦІОННОЕ БЮРО

СВИДѢТЕЛЬСТВО.

Палестинское Эмиграціонное Бюро симъ удостовѣряетъ, что предъявитель настоящаго свидѣтельства Захарій ... Ключевичъ ... лѣтъ, бѣженецъ изъ Палестины и нынѣ направляется въ Яффу

При немъ:

COMITÉ CENTRAL
DE LA FÉDÉRATION SIONISTE
BUREAU D'ÉMIGRATION
À PALESTINE

Le 9 August 1920

CERTIFICAT.

Le Bureau d'émigration auprès du Comité Central de la Fédération Sioniste de la Tauride certifie que le porteur du certificat Mr. Zacharie Klioutschewitsch age de 21 ans est refugié de Palestine et retourne à présent à Jaffa

Avec lui:

Président

Chef du Bureau

Secrétaire

תעודה

Emigration certificate issued by the Simferopol office of the Crimean Zionist Federation to enable a refugee from Palestine to return home, 1920. Courtesy Central Zionist Archives, Jerusalem.

be responsible for their maintenance for one year. About 10,000 were admitted in the first 12 months, but new regulations were issued in June 1921 specifying the categories of immigrants to be allowed to enter. The main classes were: persons of independent means, professional men, persons with definite prospects of employment, and small tradesmen and artisans with a capital of £500. Other applicants, apart from tourists, had to be approved in each case by the Immigration Department of the Palestine government. After the publication of the 1922 White Paper, permits were granted to groups of artisans and laborers selected by the Zionist Organization's Palestine Offices, the number of permits being fixed every three months by the government after negotiations with the Zionist Executive. A new Immigration Ordinance, issued in 1925 and amended in 1926 and 1927, defined the rights and functions of the Zionist Executive in regard to the Labor Schedule, which was drawn up for a six-month instead of a three-month period on the basis of an estimate of the demand for labor. It provided for the admission of the following categories:

A.(i) Persons in possession of not less than £1,000, and their families.
(ii) Professional men in possession of not less than £500.
(iii) Skilled artisans in possession of not less than £250.
(iv) Persons with an assured income of £4 per month.
B.(i) Orphans destined for institutions in Palestine.
(ii) Persons of religious occupation whose maintenance was assured.
(iii) Students whose maintenance was assured.
C. Persons who had a definite prospect of employment.
D. Dependent relatives of residents in Palestine who were in a position to maintain them.

While the Zionist Executive had to be constantly on the watch to ensure what it regarded as a fair interpretation of these definitions, the most serious differences with the administration arose over category C, which was the only one allowing for the admission of workers without means or capital of their own. As the time came round for the issue of each half-year quota, the Executive would submit a detailed estimate of the demand for labor in the existing economy and in enterprises to be set up with its aid or by private enterprise, but these were invariably slashed by the administration. The result was often a shortage of Jewish labor, which hampered economic development and caused a drift from the countryside to the towns in search of better-paid employment.

The *ḥalutzim* were the outstanding element in the 35,000 immigrants of the Third Aliyah (1919–23). They did not only find their places in the existing economic and social structure or act as passive recipients of aid from the Zionist institutions; they were a creative force, which transformed the character of the *yishuv* and played a prominent part in its leadership. Together with their predecessors of the Second Aliyah, they founded the Histadrut, the comprehensive countrywide labor organization; played a

Third Aliyah immigrants employed in constructing the Afulah–Nazareth road near their tented camp, 1920. Courtesy Central Zionist Archives, Jerusalem.

leading role in the creation of the Haganah defense organization; provided workers for the construction of housing and roads and the beginnings of industry; strengthened the foundations of Jewish agriculture; and expanded the map of Jewish settlement by establishing many kibbutzim and moshavim. To a large extent, they not only integrated themselves, but also prepared the way for others to follow.

Rise in Middle-Class Aliyah. The drop in the influx of *ḥalutzim* in 1924, mainly due to Soviet restrictions on the work of He-Ḥalutz, was compensated for by a considerable increase in middle-class immigration, bringing the influx up from some 8,000 in each of the years 1920–23 to almost 13,000 in 1924 and 33,000 in 1925. This was the start of the

Fourth Aliyah. About half the *olim* in the two latter years came from Poland, where many Jews were impoverished by an economic crisis and the anti-Jewish policy of Grabski, the finance minister (after whom this wave was often referred to as the "Grabski Aliyah"), while severe restrictions were imposed on immigration into the United States. Most of these newcomers had a little capital of their own, which they invested in small enterprises and construction of housing in the towns.

In 1926, however, the unorganized influx was halted by a severe economic crisis, and of the 13,000 who arrived in 1926 more than half left the country. These were known as *yoredim* ("descenders"—in contrast to *olim*). In the following year there was an even more serious decline to 3,000 immigrants, with nearly twice as many *yoredim;* in 1928 the number of arrivals and departures was about the same—some 2,000—and it was not until 1929 that the balance was restored, with over 5,000 *olim* and about one-third as many emigrants. This was a striking illustration of the close connection between conditions in Palestine and the rate of *aliyah.* For over a year the Zionist Executive had to pay out "doles" to the unemployed, and it was not until public works had been initiated by the government and some municipalities, and the Zionist Executive, with special funds raised in America and Britain, had started works of its own, that unemployment was reduced and the "dole" system abolished. Despite the setback, the Fourth Aliyah made an important contribution to the development of the *yishuv,* particularly in modern urbanization and the establishment of industry.

Assistance in Absorption. While the entire structure of the Jewish community in Palestine and the development of its economy was designed to facilitate the absorption of the immigrants into its cultural, social, and economic life, the Immigration Department of the Zionist Organization (later, of the Jewish Agency) undertook special measures to help the immigrants find their way. Those who had nowhere to go on arrival were generally accommodated in

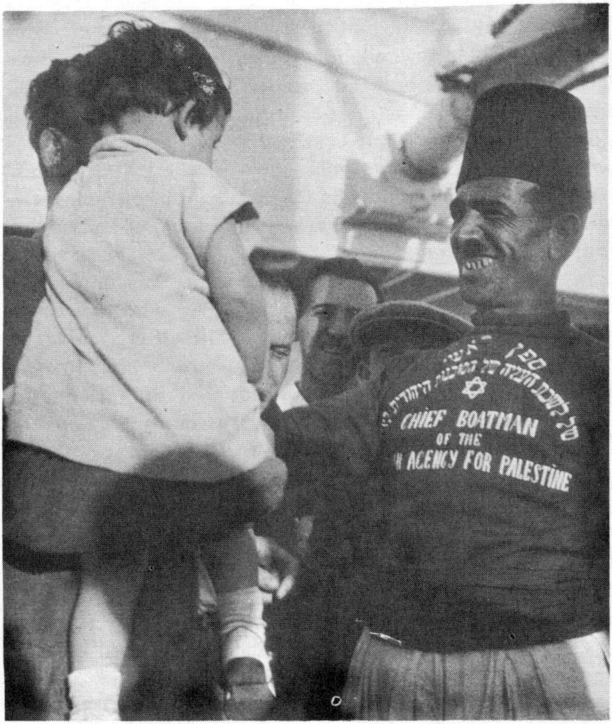

The Jewish Agency's chief boatman greeting new immigrants at Jaffa, November 1933. Courtesy Keren Hayesod, United Israel Appeal, Jerusalem.

hostels or transit camps. If their destination was a Youth Aliyah center, a kibbutz, or a moshav, they usually stayed a few days for registration and medical examination; if they were going to the moshavot or the towns, they might stay longer. The Jewish Agency provided the immigrants with health services for an initial period through the Histadrut's Kuppat Ḥolim or its own medical department. If in need of help, they were provided with bedding, clothing, and financial aid. The Jewish Agency built houses for the newcomers and subsidized various cooperative and private housing schemes. It set up small cooperative workshops for handicapped or elderly immigrants and contributed to the cost of the social welfare services of the Va'ad Le'ummi and the municipalities. It also subsidized Hebrew classes for immigrants run by the Va'ad Le'ummi, the labor organizations, and the immigrants' associations. The latter played an important role in the integration of the newcomers by dealing with special cases, acting as liaison with the Jewish institutions, and supplying loans, housing grants, etc.

The vital importance of *aliyah* for the individuals concerned, as well as for the movement as a whole, gave rise to frequent controversies. The Revisionists and other parties complained of discrimination against their members in the allocation of immigration certificates by the Zionist Palestine Offices. Various groups and individuals resorted to a variety of methods to overcome the British restrictions on *aliyah*, which were regarded as violating intrinsic Jewish rights. Many entered as tourists and remained without permission when their legal period of stay was over. To enable penniless immigrants to enter as "capitalists," they were provided with fictitious deposits of £1,000; formal marriages were arranged to enable two to enter on one certificate; some succeeded in crossing the border surreptitiously from Lebanon, Syria, or via Transjordan. In 1934 the first attempt was made to send over an immigrant ship without the permission of the authorities. In Palestine, Jews, including some in the British government service, regarded it as a national duty to help these immigrants. It is estimated that some 50,000 arrived in such ways between 1920 and 1937. The British government made strenuous efforts to prevent this "illegal" immigration and from time to time deducted the estimated number of "illegals" from the regular immigration quotas.

Political Struggle for Aliyah. The establishment in August 1929 of the enlarged Jewish Agency (based on Article 4 of the Mandate, which called upon the Zionist

Organization to take steps "to secure the cooperation of all Jews who are willing to assist in the establishment of the Jewish National Home") extended the responsibility for the Jewish enterprise in Palestine in principle to Jewry as a whole. A brilliant array of distinguished Jews from Europe and the Americas took part in its founding conference, at which a joint Executive was elected under the presidency of Chaim Weizmann. The expected expansion was held up, however, by the outbreak of Arab violence in the following month and the political struggle of the next two years. *Aliyah* was the major practical issue of this struggle and the touchstone of Britain's capacity to carry out the fundamental provisions of the Mandate. The Zionist Organization had accepted the principle that immigration should be regulated according to the economic absorptive capacity of Palestine, while conducting a continuous struggle with the administration over the interpretation and implementation of the principle. But when Lord Passfield, the British colonial secretary, imposed political restrictions on *aliyah,* as well as limitations of Jewish land purchases, in surrender to Arab violence, the Zionist Organization and the *yishuv* regarded this as a blow to the future of the Jewish National Home, and Weizmann resigned from the presidency of the Zionist Organization in protest. The struggle against the Passfield White Paper was ultimately crowned with success, however, and the MacDonald letter of February 1931, which effectively nullified the White Paper restrictions, reestablished the political conditions for further development and progress.

It was none too soon. Dark clouds were gathering over European Jewry. The worldwide economic crisis was having an increasing effect on the Jews of Eastern and Central Europe; anti-Semitism was spreading and sharpening; the star of Hitler was in the ascendant in Germany; and at the same time immigration restrictions in the countries not so severely affected were tightening. For millions of Jews in Eastern Europe, in the poignant words of Chaim Weizmann to the Peel Commission[15] in 1936, the world was divided into "places where they cannot live" and "places which they cannot enter." The only place of refuge was Palestine, where a Jewish community of over 200,000 (in 1933), was ready to welcome them.

In the Shadow of Nazism. Between 1933, the year of Hitler's rise to power, and 1936, 164,000 *olim* arrived in Palestine; 24,000 of them were citizens of Germany, in addition to nationals of other countries and "stateless" individuals who had been living there. About a quarter of the immigrants arrived with "capitalist" immigration certificates and the £31,570,000 brought in during the period by private investors was about ten times as much as the total contributed by fund-raising organizations.

Almost a quarter of this sum came through a special arrangement between the Jewish Agency and the German

A clerk in the Zionist Office in Berlin interviewing a prospective immigrant, 1935. Courtesy Central Zionist Archives, Jerusalem.

[15]Commission appointed by the British government under chairmanship of Lord Peel, which recommended the partition of Palestine

authorities for the transfer (Haavara) of German-Jewish capital. Under this agreement, emigrants from Germany obtained their first £1,000 in cash so that they could get their immigration certificates and deposited the rest of their assets with a clearinghouse in Berlin; the sterling equivalent was recovered after arrival from a second clearinghouse in Palestine, to which Jewish merchants made their payments for goods imported from Germany, while the German exporters were paid in Berlin. Moneys collected for the Jewish national funds and various other remittances to Palestine were also transferred through Haavara. The arrangement was fiercely criticized as a breach of the worldwide Jewish boycott of German goods, but it was strongly defended on the ground that it was the only way to salvage the property of German Jews. The 19th Zionist Congress, which met at Lucerne in 1935 and which paid special attention to the plight of German Jewry, approved the agreement but ruled that it be placed under the control of the Executive.

In 1933 a new type of immigration, called Youth Aliyah, was started to enable boys and girls to be looked after in educational institutions and villages in Palestine. The government issued special immigration certificates for them on the basis of guarantees given by the Jewish authorities. The work was largely financed by Hadassah and organized by its leader, Henrietta Szold. Up to the outbreak of the war, 5,000 young people were saved in this way (70% of them from Germany, 20% from Austria, and the rest from Czechoslovakia, Poland, and Rumania see Table 5); another 15,000 were brought over to Britain and the Scandinavian countries. (See also Ch. 7.)

The German and Austrian Jews made an important contribution to the progress of the *yishuv*. They constituted the first large-scale influx from Western and Central Europe, and their skills and experience raised business standards and improved urban amenities. A relatively high proportion of them practiced medicine or one of the other professions, and they provided a majority of the musicians who formed the new Philharmonic Orchestra, as well as a considerable part of its audiences.

Immigration again dropped, however, in 1936, when the Arab revolt began. On of its major demands was the stoppage of Jewish immigration, and the Peel Commission, while proposing the partition of Palestine and the establishment of a Jewish state, also recommended that the government should fix a "political high level" of 12,000 Jewish immigrants a year for the next five years, irrespective of the country's economic absorptive capacity. In August 1937, a new Immigration Ordinance was issued empowering the high commissioner "temporarily" to fix a maximum aggregate number of immigrants for any specified period, as well as the maximum number to be admitted in any category. For the eight-month period up to March 1938, not more than 8,000 Jews were to be allowed in. From March 31, 1939, the ordinance was given general validity, despite the increasing intensity and range of the persecution of the Jews in Europe. The Zionist movement bitterly protested against the imposition of the "political high level" and denounced it as a violation of one of the most fundamental provisions of the Mandate.

The sufferings inflicted on the German Jews by the Nazi regime attracted worldwide attention, and in 1938 President Roosevelt called an international conference at Evian to seek homes for the refugees. The dismal failure of the conference, which was not allowed to consider Palestine, showed that no one was ready to welcome them but the *yishuv*. The Jewish Agency submitted to the conference a plan for the rapid and constructive absorption of 100,000 refugees in Palestine, but the Jewish National Home was not permitted to perform its most vitally important function at the very time when it was most desperately needed. Immigration had dropped from some 27,000 in 1936 to 9,400 in the following year, and, although it rose slightly to 11,200 in 1938 and 13,700 in 1939, it was far too little to save the Jews of Europe. The British White Paper of 1939 went a long way to meeting Arab demands for the

Veterans of the Jewish Legion in a Jerusalem protest march against the British White Paper of May 1939. Courtesy Keren Hayesod, United Israel Appeal, Jerusalem.

artificial limitation of Jewish immigration, which was regarded as the major instrument for establishing the Jewish National Home, and envisioned the stoppage of its future development by making further immigration at the end of the five years dependent on Arab consent. The *yishuv*, supported by Jews in the Diaspora and many non-Jewish sympathizers, denounced the White Paper as a betrayal of Britain's obligations under the Mandate. The organization of "illegal" immigration was intensified, and more and more refugee ships made their way to Palestine.

4 "ILLEGAL" IMMIGRATION AND THE BERIḤAH

"Illegal" Immigration. "Illegal" ships had been sent by He-Ḥalutz, bringing pioneering youth, and later by the Revisionists and some individuals, who brought out large numbers of Central and East European Jews, sometimes in collusion with their governments. It was known in the *yishuv* as "Aliyah Bet" ("B Aliyah"). At first this activity was frowned upon by the Jewish authorities, but in 1938, when British restrictions were maintained despite the growing and urgent needs, the underground Mosad le-Aliyah Bet ("Institute for Aliyah Bet"), headed by Shaul Avigur, took the lead on behalf of the Haganah and the Jewish Agency. Between July 1934 and the outbreak of war in September 1939, 43 ships succeeded in disembarking over 15,000 refugee passengers on the shores of Palestine. The *yishuv* and the Zionist movement did not regard these Jews—most of whom were refugees from poverty, persecution, and, as the event showed, death—as "illegal immigrants"; for them the Mandatory government's attempts to stop them entering the Jewish National Home were illegal. They were referred to as *ma'pilim* ("trail-blazers" or "daring pioneers").

Of the Jews trapped in Europe by the outbreak of war in September 1939, only a few thousand managed to escape the impending catastrophe. It was desperately difficult to get ships, fuel, supplies, and crews willing to risk the voyage in wartime conditions. Legal immigration had declined to a trickle, and those who landed without getting permission in advance, which was seldom possible, were still treated as illegal immigrants. The British navy kept constant watch.

The captain of the "illegal" immigration ship *Atrato* addressing his passengers, 1939. Courtesy Haganah Historical Archives,

Some of the refugee boats were fired on as they approached the coasts. Some were turned back: three of these sank, and only the human cargo of one of them (the *Pancho* in May 1940) was saved from drowning. The passengers on the others were interned in camps or deported to British colonies. The refugees were embarked at ports in the Balkan countries, and some of them landed at Constantinople, whence they made their way by land to Palestine. Twenty-one boats in all completed the voyage, carrying some 15,000 refugees, whose numbers were deducted from the official quotas. There was also some "illegal" immigration overland by Jews from Iraq, Syria, and Lebanon across the northern border.

In the summer of 1943, after the world had learned of the Nazi Holocaust, the British government instructed its embassy in Turkey to give entry permits to Palestine to Jews who succeeded in escaping from Nazi-occupied Europe. The emissaries of the Haganah, including those who were parachuted into enemy territory, did all they could to facilitate the flight of the refugees. From the beginning of 1944 they were assisted by the United States, which set up

Young refugees from Germany **dancing** the *hora* after disembarking at Tel Aviv, April 1939. Courtesy Keren Hayesod, United Israel Appeal, Jerusalem.

the War Refugee Board for the purpose. Altogether, some 61,000 persons entered Palestine, with or without immigration certificates, during the years 1940–45.

The Beriḥah. At the end of World War II, tens of thousands of Jews found that they could not remain in the countries of Central Europe either because of their memories of the Holocaust and the destruction of their homes or because of the anti-Semitic atmosphere that prevailed in these countries. A mass migration of the remnants of the Holocaust began. It was partially spontaneous and partially organized as an attempt to find a way to reach Palestine. The first initiators of the organized Beriḥah (meaning "flight") were leaders of Jewish resistance groups, partisans, and organizers of Zionist underground groups who already had participated in illegal border crossings in Nazi-occupied Eastern Europe during the war years.

In 1944, with the liberation of Rovno in Volhynia and Vilna by the Soviet Army in February and April, respectively, illegal groups of former Jewish partisans were formed independently of each other. Their aim was to take out the remnants of the Jewish population and bring them to Ereẓ Israel. They were joined by Zionist groups returning from Soviet Asia, and met in Lublin in December 1944 under the leadership of Abba Kovner. In January 1945, they were joined by the remnants of the Warsaw ghetto fighters under Itzhak Cukierman, and founded the Beriḥah organization under the leadership of Kovner. The first groups were sent to Rumania in the middle of January 1945, in the hope of reaching Ereẓ Israel with the help of emissaries (*sheliḥim*) of the *yishuv* staying at the time in Bucharest. During the first months after the war, before the borders of Central European countries were redrawn and closed and when millions of Displaced Persons were returning to their homes, the movement of Jews searching for a way to Palestine also began. An event connected with this mass movement was the "Rescue Train," which, under the auspices of the International Red Cross, set out for Poland to return to Rumania Jews who had been deported by the Germans. This project succeeded in returning from Poland to Rumania about 5,000 Jews, including many children. But hopes of reaching Palestine from Rumania soon had to be discarded, and in May, Kovner had instead established transit points in Hungary and Yugoslavia, moving his people toward Italy, which he himself reached in July. Polish Jews were now coming via Slovakia to Budapest, and thence to Graz in Austria, hoping to cross the Italian border from there. In August, however, the British occupation forces stationed there closed the border and 12,000 people were stranded in the Graz area. They managed to cross the border in small groups only in the winter of 1945/46.

A center (*Merkaz la-Golah*) for smuggling Jews into Italy from the liberated concentration camps in Germany and Austria was established by Palestinian Jewish soldiers stationed in Europe, both from the Jewish Brigade and from other army units. It started its activities in June 1945 and brought in some 15,000 people till August, when British forces sealed the border. Financing in this early period was from Jewish Agency funds. The first attempt to organize the migration of Jewish survivors throughout Europe was made at a meeting of Beriḥah activists in Bratislava in March 1946. A central committee of the Beriḥah was chosen with Mordechai Surkis from the Jewish Brigade and Pinḥas Rashish, head of the Palestine aid delegation to Poland, as its heads. This committee exercised an ill-defined and shadowy control over Beriḥah activities in Europe until the end of 1946.

From August 1945 onward, a movement started out of Poland into the Displaced Persons (DP) camps of Czechoslovakia; the various routes led to the U.S. zone in Austria and into Bavaria. From October onward an alternative route operated via Szczeczyn (Stettin), Berlin, and the British zone (northern Germany) to the U.S. zone in the south. Transit through Czechoslovakia, Austria, and Hungary was controlled by Levi Kopelevich (Argov), a *shali'aḥ* from Palestine, who from March 1946 headed the Beriḥah secretariat in Bratislava. Movements were coordinated with the Beriḥah in Poland under Isser Ben-Ẓvi, a *shali'aḥ* who had taken over in October 1945. In the winter of 1945/46, funds began to be received from the American Jewish Joint Distribution Committee for food and clothing for stranded refugees. The control over Beriḥah exercised heretofore through Surkis was now acknowledged to be in the hands of the Mosad le-Aliyah Bet for "illegal" immigration in Palestine, whose head, Shaul Avigur, moved his office to Paris in 1946.

The movement was largely organized by Zionist youth movements whose representatives in Poland formed the Beriḥah "center," to which the commander was responsible. The movements and Zionist parties formed groups, many of which were influenced by the kibbutz idea and therefore known as "kibbutzim." The groups were directed to border towns where Beriḥah teams accommodated them in "stores" (temporary lodgings). There they were provided with slips of paper containing a code *("parol")* and sent to the actual border station ("point") where the local Beriḥah team smuggled them across. Until 1946, forged Red Cross documents were employed to identify people as Greek refugees. In Czechoslovakia, an informal agreement was obtained not to hamper the movement of Jews, and UNRRA and the Czech government paid the train fares from the Polish border to either Bratislava or As on the Czech-German frontier. On the Szczeczyn-Berlin route, Soviet or Polish truck drivers were bribed into smuggling people in, and exit from Berlin to the British zone was effected either through UNRRA officials whose sympathy was obtained or with the help of forged documents. From October 1945 onward, the operation in Austria was under Asher Ben-Nathan, and in Germany under Ephraim Frank, both *sheliḥim* from Palestine. In Vienna a series of transit camps were clustered around the Rothschild Hospital, receiving refugees passing from Bratislava to the U.S. zone of Austria. From the U.S. zone of Austria transit was effected either to Italy (until about May 1946), directed by Issachar Haimovich, or to the U.S. zone in Germany.

The U.S. Army did not encourage entry of Jewish refugees into their zones. However, poor conditions in DP camps in these zones had caused an investigation to be made by Earl G. Harrison in August, 1945, and the report that was published on Sept. 30, 1945, reflected badly on the army. To avoid arousing public opinion in the United

States the army acquiesced in Jewish refugee movements, provided no very large numbers were involved. Simon H. Rifkind and Philip S. Bernstein, advisers on Jewish affairs to the U.S. command in Germany, played a large part in persuading the army to maintain its tolerant attitude.

The murder of 41 Jews in a pogrom at Kielce (Poland) on July 4, 1946, created a wave of panic among Polish Jews, who now included the 150,000 repatriates from the U.S.S.R. who came out from February 1946 onward (before that there had been only 80,000 Jews in Poland). Pressure was exerted on Beriḥah by panic-stricken Jews to take them out of Poland. In July this was still done by the usual illegal means. But the Polish government, which arrived at the conclusion that it would not be able to restrain the outbursts against the Jews, saw their exodus from Poland as a solution to the problem. In late July, negotiations conducted by Itzhak Cukierman with Polish government agencies led to an oral understanding whereby Jews were allowed to leave Poland without hindrance through the Silesian border into Czechoslovakia. Simultaneously (on July 26) the Czech government, largely through the influence of Jan Masaryk, the foreign minister, decided to open its frontier to Jews fleeing from Poland. In the three months of July, August, and September 1946 more than 70,000 Jews fled through Czechoslovakia. Transport was paid for by the Czechs, against an UNRRA promise to return the money later; food was obtained largely from the JDC and UNRRA. The exodus of those months was joined by 15,000 Hungarian Jews and some 1,000 Rumanian and Czech Jews. Despite Polish insistence that only the Silesian route should be used after the July agreement, Beriḥah continued to send also large numbers of Jews via Szczeczyn to Berlin, a route which was controlled by Jewish Brigade soldiers. Others went from Szczeczyn to Luebeck and Hanover in the British zone by train or boat through PUR, the Polish agency expelling Germans from Poland: the Jews posed as Germans and were thus enabled to leave by "being expelled." The total number leaving Poland from July 1945 to October 1946 was estimated at 110,000, excluding PUR and a large number of people who came out not with the organized Beriḥah but with professional smugglers, Jews as well as non-Jews. From the beginnings of the Beriḥah until October 1946 no less than 180,000 people were involved in the migratory movements.

After some hesitation, and due again largely to the intervention of Rabbi Philip Bernstein, the U.S. Army allowed the large scale move into the U.S. zones of Germany and Austria to take place in the summer of 1946. Movements out of Germany into Italy were limited, especially during the second half of 1946, until the route was reestablished in early 1947 through the Valle Aurina. In early 1947 the Polish government terminated the arrangement at the border; movement via Szczeczyn had almost come to a standstill in November 1946. During 1947, less than 10,000 Jews managed to leave Poland via Beriḥah routes. In Germany, Beriḥah cooperated with the committees of Jewish DPs to arrange for social and political absorption of the refugees into the camps. Beriḥah's orientation was clearly Zionist, but there were refugees who declared their preference for migration to countries other than Palestine.

The Beriḥah movement from the Soviet Union was a special case. Many Jews who had lived in prewar Poland left the U.S.S.R. with their families as part of the Polish repatriation program. The position of veteran citizens of the Soviet Union was a more difficult one. Nonetheless, activities of the Beriḥah were organized by a number of bodies, which, inter alia, brought out many Lubavich Ḥasidim from the Soviet Union. When the new Soviet border was definitely sealed in 1946, the Soviet authorities began to seize the Beriḥah organizers, some of whom were arrested and sentenced to long prison terms. At the end of 1946 a meeting of Beriḥah commanders was held at Basle during the 22nd Zionist Congress. Shaul Avigur, head of the Mosad, was present. There a new European commander of the Beriḥah, Ephraim Dekel, a former head of Haganah Intelligence in Palestine, was nominated. Under Dekel Beriḥah became more closely linked with the Mosad, but the numbers coming in from Eastern Europe were falling. In the spring of 1947 economic crisis and fear of anti-Semitism caused a panic flight of some 15,000 Rumanian Jews to Hungary and Austria. On April 21, 1947, the U.S. Army decreed that no more Jews would be accepted into existing DP camps, but Beriḥah poured the refugees into the Viennese transit camps until the American authorities relented and allowed the people entrance into camps in the U.S. zone in contravention of the decree. The tension in Palestine between the Haganah and the dissident underground organizations, Irgun Ẓeva'i Le'ummi (I.Ẓ.L.) and Loḥamei Ḥerut Israel (Leḥi), sometimes influenced the work of the Beriḥah as well, and in September 1947 a Beriḥah man was murdered at a "point" near Innsbruck by I.Ẓ.L. members. In general, however, the Revisionists were part of the current of the Beriḥah and the "illegal" immigration to Palestine.

In 1948, Meir Sapir took over from Dekel as Beriḥah commander, and Beriḥah was slowly wound up, though Beriḥah points still operated on certain eastern borders in 1949. In the west, Beriḥah points existed on the German-French and, briefly, on the Belgian, frontier, and the *Exodus* passengers (see below) passed through in June 1947. However, entry into France was regulated by the Mosad rather than Beriḥah. The total number of people who left Eastern Europe between 1944 and 1948 can be estimated at about 250,000, and of these about 80% at least came with the organized Beriḥah. The Beriḥah was a prime factor in the struggle for the establishment of the Jewish State from 1945 to 1948. It dramatically underscored President Truman's demand for a speedy admission of 100,000 Jewish refugees to Palestine (August 1945) and was reflected in the conclusions of the Anglo-American Committee (May 1946). It created a reservoir of people from which came the masses of immigrants that fought together with the *yishuv* to open the gates of Palestine to

Jewish immigration and to establish the State of Israel.

"Illegal" Immigration after World War II. Parallel to the Beriḥah, large-scale operations at sea were resumed by the Mosad after the war, the immigrants being mainly refugee survivors of European Jewry who had reached the shores of Italy, France, Rumania, Yugoslavia, and Greece. Their passage was supervised by Mosad emissaries, the immigrants in most cases embarking at small, remote ports, and traveling under cramped conditions in densely packed vessels, most of which were unfit for passenger transportation. The Italians and others who at first constituted the crews of these ships were later joined by Palestinian and American Jews. The refugees were escorted by members of the Haganah and volunteers from the Diaspora, particularly from the U.S. The success of the operation was due in no small measure to the manner in which the refugees themselves, regardless of age or sex, willingly endured privation and danger, and to the total solidarity of the *yishuv* with the refugees. Haganah members and others received boats which arrived clandestinely at night to desolate places of the sea shore, carrying on their shoulders those who were unable to wade to the shore—the elderly, the sick, women, and children. In other cases the refugees were immediately brought in buses and trucks to kibbutzim and having changed their clothes could not be recognized as such by the searching British police.

In the years from 1945 to 1948, 65 immigrant boats embarked for Palestine, all under the aegis of the Mosad, save for one boat dispatched by the Hebrew National Liberation Committee founded by Revisionists in the U. S. Most of these were intercepted by the British; among the few that succeeded in landing their passengers were the *Dalin* (August 1945), the *Hanna Szenes* (December 1945), and the *Shabbetai Lozinski,* which went aground on the rocks near Ashdod in March 1947, the immigrants mingling with hundreds of local residents who came to their rescue so that the authorities might not distinguish between them. Intercepted boats were impounded and the passengers transferred to a detention camp at Athlit, some of them later being released within the framework of the limited immigration quota. From August 1946 the British began deporting the clandestine immigrants to detention camps in Cyprus, where 51,500 were kept under detention and 2,000 children were born. The detainees were by no means passive. They organized themselves and prepared for settlement in Ereẓ Israel with the aid of emissaries from there, learning Hebrew, and even undergoing military training. Seven hundred and fifty of the detainees, chosen by their own committees, were allowed to enter Palestine every month, the number being deducted from the official immigration quota, but the majority reached Israel only after independence, between May 1948 and February 1949.

The critical moment for all the immigrant ships was that of their interception by the British patrol boats, which were ready to attack if their orders were not obeyed. The methods of attack ranged from ramming the boats to using tear gas, batons, and, at times, firearms in order to overcome the immigrants' resistance. The men in charge had to decide on the measure of resistance to be offered, according to such factors as the age and condition of the passengers: sometimes the attackers were met with sticks, stones, and tins of preserves; generally, passive resistance was offered to the British soldiers, who dragged the immigrants to the deportation boats. Many were injured and several died in these encounters. Among the ships whose passengers offered the strongest resistance were the *Latrun* (October 1946), the *Keneset Yisrael* (November 1946), the *Chaim Arlosoroff* (February 1947), and the *Theodor Herzl* (April 1947). In March 1946 the British Army prevailed on the Italian authorities to prevent the departure from La Spezia harbor of the 1,014 refugees on board the *Dov Hos* and the *Eliyahu Golomb;* the immigrants reacted by declaring a hunger strike which aroused world public opinion and compelled Britain to permit the boats to reach Palestine.

Clandestine immigration was the spur to and a focal

issue of the resistance movement against the "White Paper" regime. Mass demonstrations were held in Palestine on behalf of the refugees, frequently ending in bloody clashes with the military authorities. The Athlit internment camp was penetrated by a Haganah unit and internees released (October 1945); members of the Palmaḥ sabotaged installations involved in the detention and arrest of clandestine immigrants, damaging British deportation boats and coastguard and radar stations.

The struggle for the right of free immigration reached its peak in summer 1947, when 4,515 refugees on board the *Exodus 1947* reached the shores of Palestine. After the fight with the British on board (three killed, 28 injured), the passengers were removed from the *Exodus* to three transports which took them to France, but the French government refused to take them off the British deportation boat against their will, while the refugees themselves chose to endure the intense discomfort of their stifling cramped quarters in the summer heat rather than disembark. They were finally taken to Hamburg, where they were forcibly removed and transferred to a British internment camp in Germany. This incident aroused world opinion against Britain's policy of closing the gates of Palestine to survivors of the Holocaust. One of the last clandestine immigration operations was a convoy of two large boats, the *Pan York* and *Pan Crescent,* transporting more than 15,000 Jews, the majority from Rumania, which left Bulgaria at the end of 1947 despite British and U.S. attempts to prevent their setting sail. The passengers were interned in the Cyrus detention camps.

The urgent problem of the Holocaust survivors, which could only be solved in Palestine, had aroused the movement and the *yishuv* to greater exertions and stiffened their determination to fight the British policy of continued restrictions. At the same time it was a striking demonstration to the world of the central importance of the Jewish National Home for the Jewish people and the inadequacy of the Mandate, as interpreted by the British government, to provide an answer. The arrival of the refugee boats and

Polish refugee children arrive in Ereẓ Israel by way of Teheran, February, 1943. Courtesy Keren Hayesod, United Israel Appeal, Jerusalem.

the treatment of their passengers by the British did more than anything else to arouse world sympathy for the Zionist cause. The demand for the admission of 100,000 Jews, supported by U.S. President Truman and later by the Anglo-American Committee on Palestine, was a major focus of the Zionist struggle. The visits paid by the U.N. Special Committee on Palestine to the D.P.[16] camps and the determination expressed by the survivors of the Holocaust to accept no solution but *aliyah* were major factors in persuading the committee that the Mandatory regime must be ended and a Jewish state established.

Table 1. Immigration, 1882–May 14, 1948

Year	Immigrants[1]	Rate[2]	Year	Immigrants[1]	Rate[2]
1882–1914	55–70,000		1934	45,267	177
			1935	66,472	206
1919	1,806	32	1936	29,595	80
1920	8,223	135	1937	10,629	27
1921	8,294	115	1938	14,675	36
1922	8,685	104	1939	31,195	72
1923	8,175	91	1940	10,643	23
1924	13,892	146	1941	4,592	10
1925	34,386	285	1942	4,206	9
1926	13,855	93	1943	10,063	20
1927	3,034	20	1944	15,552	30
1928	2,178	14	1945	15,259	28
1929	5,249	34	1946	18,760	32
1930	4,944	30	1947	22,098	36
1931	4,075	24	June 1–May 14, 1948	17,165	73
1932	12,553	69			
1933	37,337	177			

[1] Including immigrants without visas and tourists who settled.
[2] Immigrants per 1,000 of the Jewish population.

During the entire period of the Mandate, some 483,000 Jews had settled in Palestine—almost six times the size of the Jewish population at the beginning of the period. Almost 88% had come from Europe, where the Zionist movement was strong and the pressure of persecution was great, including 39.6% from Poland, 14.2% from Germany and Austria, 12.2% from the Soviet Union, Lithuania, and Latvia, and 4.1% from the Balkan countries. Less than 2%

[16] Jewish Displaced Persons as a result of World War II

The *Exodus 1947* on its arrival in Haifa **after the** skirmish between the "illegal" immigrants and British soldiers, July 18, 1947. Courtesy Keren Hayesod, United Israel Appeal,

came from the Americas, and some 10.4% from Asia and Africa, which for some time had been outside the mainstream of the development of Zionism.

5 STATE OF ISRAEL (1948–72)

"Ingathering of the Exiles" Begins. The departure of the British and the assumption of sovereignty by the State of Israel, radically transformed the nature of *aliyah*. The first of Israel's aims, as defined in the Declaration of Independence, was: "The State of Israel shall be open to Jewish immigration and the ingathering of the exiles." The first act of the newly constituted Provisional Council of State was the abolition of all previous restrictions on Jewish immigration: the only limitations henceforward were to be the readiness of Jews to come, their freedom to leave, and the facilities for transporting them; absorptive capacity was taken for granted. The way was open for the realization of the prophetic dream of the ingathering of the exiles, i.e., the return to the homeland of all Jews who were willing and able to come and the transfer of complete Jewish communities within a short space of time. This national purpose was given legislative expression in the Law of Return 1950, which granted every Jew the automatic right to become an *oleh*, i.e., to settle permanently in Israel, and the Citizenship Law, 1952, which enabled every *oleh* to become a citizen as soon as he set foot on Israel soil. At an early stage, it was decided that immigration and absorption should be the joint tasks of the State of Israel and Jewry in the Diaspora. The World Zionist Organization, represented by the Jewish Agency, was therefore charged to encourage and organize immigration and assist in the absorption of the immigrants in close cooperation and coordination with the government of Israel. The terms of these responsibilities and functions were set down in the World Zionist Organization-Jewish Agency Status Law, 1952, which recognized the Zionist Organization-Jewish Agency as representing Diaspora Jews in all matters concerning immigration and absorption. In 1954 a Covenant was signed by the government and the Agency, further defining the latter's functions and methods of coordinating their activities.

Between May 15, 1948, and the end of 1972, over 1,400,000 Jews—twice as many as the Jewish population at the end of the Mandate—settled in Israel. They started coming as soon as the State was established. First to arrive were the 25,000 "illegal" immigrants detained by the British in Cyprus: within a few short weeks, they were all brought over. During May–August 1948, while the War of Liberation was raging, 33,000 immigrants came in; then the pace quickened and 70,000 arrived during September–December, mostly survivors of the Holocaust from the displaced persons' camps in Germany, Austria, and Italy. In the next four months, January–April 1949, the number of immigrants reached 100,000. In all, 203,000 Jews from 42

Escape tunnel at the Cyprus detention camp. Courtesy Central Zionist Archives, Jerusalem.

Arrival of the first "legal" immigrants to Israel, two days after the declaration of the State, May 17, 1948. Courtesy Keren Hayesod, United Israel Appeal, Jerusalem.

countries arrived in the first year of independence. This mass immigration continued until the end of 1951. During this period entire Jewish communities were transplanted to Israel, producing drastic changes in the map of Diaspora Jewry. More than 37,000 of Bulgaria's 45,000 Jews came; 30,500 of Libya's 35,000; all but about 1,000 of the 45,000 in Yemen; 121,512 of the 130,000 in Iraq; two-thirds (103,732) of Polish Jewry; and one-third (118,940) of the Jews in Rumania. The D.P. camps in Europe could be closed because their inmates had gone to Israel. This mass immigration was marked by unexpected and dramatic events, when the Jewish Agency had to improvise the movement of tens of thousands of people within a very short time and in adverse conditions. These migrations were organized as special operations, planned and executed by special emissaries. The most dramatic were Operation Magic Carpet, for the Yemenite Jews, and Operation Ezra and Nehemiah, which brought over Iraqi Jewry.

Thousands of Yemenite Jews, gripped by messianic enthusiasm, had been making their way south on foot,

Yemenites on their way to Israel in "Operation Magic Carpet," 1949. Courtesy American Joint Distribution Committee,

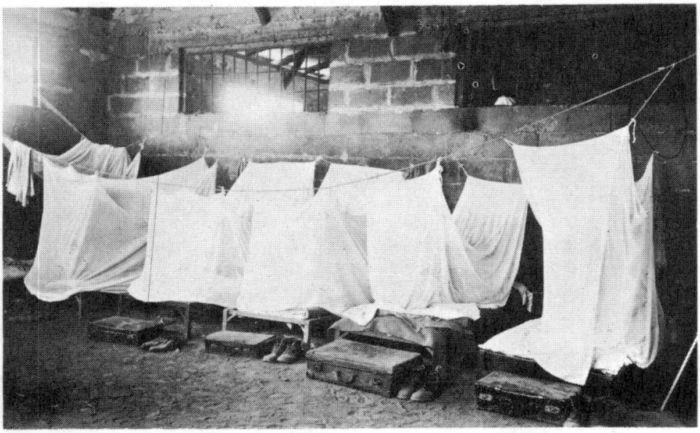

New settlers sleeping under mosquito nets in an abandoned building at Arida (now Sedeh Eliyahu).

Table 2. Mass Immigration, May 1948—December 1951.

All Countries	684,201
Eastern Europe	
Rumania	118,940
Poland	103,732
Bulgaria	37,231
Czechoslovakia	18,217
Hungary	13,631
Yugoslavia	7,595
Soviet Union (Lithuania, Latvia)	4,698
Total	304,044
Western Europe	
Germany	8,856
France	4,008
Austria	2,994
Greece	2,005
Britain	2,143
Italy	1,415
Belgium	1,108
Netherlands	1,102
Spain	412
Sweden	429
Switzerland	386
Other European Countries	147
Total	25,005
Asia	
Iraq	121,512
Turkey	34,213
Iran	24,804
Aden	3,155
India	2,337
China	2,167
Cyprus	136
Yemen	45,199
Other Countries	3,700
Total	237,223

Africa	
Morocco	30,750
Tunisia	13,139
Algeria	1,523
Libya	30,482
South Africa	584
Ethiopia	83
Egypt	16,508
Other Countries	108
Total	93,177
Western Hemisphere	
United States	1,909
Canada	233
Argentina	1,134
Brazil	442
Other Latin American Countries	870
Total	4,588
Australia	171
Unregistered	19,993

carrying their scanty belongings, to the British colony of Aden. On the establishment of independence, Jewish Agency representatives started negotiations with the imam of Yemen, the local sultans and sheikhs, and the British authorities, and in May 1949 agreement was reached. Although the Jews of Yemen were not forced to leave, almost the entire community made the long and arduous trek to Aden, whence they were brought to Israel in an intensive large-scale airlift. About 47,000 were thus transported "on eagles' wings" (Ex. 19:4) and by the end of 1950, when the operation was concluded, only a few hundred remained.

In March 1950, the Iraqi government suddenly enacted a "Special Law Authorizing the Emigration of Jews" providing they renounced their citizenship in writing. Those above the age of 20 were permitted to take out a sum equal to some $16 each; young people up to 20 and children up to 12 could take only $10 and $6 respectively. Many Jews had to sell their property in haste for pitiful sums not in any proportion to its real value, but they could not take out the proceeds. The Jewish Agency immediately made emergency arrangements to move the Iraqi Jews to Israel. They were flown to Cyprus and then brought to Israel by air or sea, the whole operation being completed within 18 months.

All in all, 684,201 immigrants—more than the entire Jewish population the day independence was proclaimed—came between May 15, 1948, and the end of 1951.

Absorbing the First Wave. *Aliyah* was the lifeblood of the new state, but it was only the beginning of the process of integrating veterans and newcomers from a hundred countries into one nation. The second stage was *kelitah* ("absorption"), a word that denoted a multitude of tasks: collecting the immigrants at the port or airfield; providing them with food and lodging; building temporary and permanent housing; finding employment; expanding health services; organizing education. Complete absorption was a task that affected all areas of the country's life and demanded massive financial participation by Diaspora Jewry through the Jewish Agency. In one year the Agency's staff had to transport 200,000 immigrants from the point of arrival to their new homes. In the first place, most of them were taken to Sha'ar ha-Aliyah ("Gateway of Aliyah"), near Haifa, a converted British army camp, where they were registered, medically examined, inoculated and vaccinated, classified, and sent on to their destinations. An average of 1,000 a day passed through Sha'ar ha-Aliyah at peak.

At first large numbers were accommodated in dwellings abandoned by the Arabs who had fled during the War of Independence. A national immigrant housing corporation, Amidar, was established in 1949, and by the end of 1951 28,000 homes had been built. At the same time prefabricated huts were imported from Sweden. Some went to villages of various types and a number were received by relatives, who helped them to find housing and employment. All these expedients, however, were not sufficient to accommodate the influx and many of them had to be sent to camps—some converted from British army quarters—where they were fed and looked after until homes and work could be found for them. Those who needed to know Hebrew to work in their professions were sent to ulpanim, special language courses using intensive modern methods, the first of which was set up in 1949.

More than two-thirds of the 393,197 immigrants who arrived during two critical years, from May 1948 to May 1950, were settled in towns and villages: 123,669 were accommodated in houses abandoned by Arabs and 53,000 in permanent housing in towns and villages; 36,497 were helped by relatives to find homes and work; 35,700 settled in newly established moshavim and 16,000 in kibbutzim; and 6,000 children were placed in Youth Aliyah institutions. Less than one-third—112,015 persons—remained in immigration camps and temporary housing while no information was available with regard to 9,596.

As the pressure of immigration increased, the camps were filled to capacity. The overcrowding and enforced idleness, without work for the adults or decent conditions for their families, were demoralizing and it became urgently necessary to find better methods of dealing with those for whom permanent housing was not yet available. The immediate solution, devised in 1950, was the *ma'barah*, the transitional camp or quarter, in which the newcomers were provided with work and made responsible for looking after themselves. Some of the large camps were closed down; others were converted into *ma'barot* by closing the communal dining hall and providing each family with facilities for buying and cooking its own meals. In addition, *ma'barot* were specially built near the towns or in other places where work was available in the neighborhood. At first some of them consisted of tents, but these were soon replaced by canvas-walled huts or tin shacks. In each *ma'barah* there were wooden huts for the labor exchange, clinic, school, and kindergarten. The construction of a large

Ma'barah in Tiberias, December 1951. Courtesy Keren Hayesod, United Israel Appeal, Jerusalem.

ma'barah took not more than a few weeks and thus thousands of immigrants were given temporary shelter within a short period. By May 1952 there were 113 *ma'barot* with a population of 250,000.

For those who could not, as yet, find employment special relief-work projects were organized in afforestation, clearing and reclamation of land, weed-removing and other agricultural work, and road construction. Many such schemes were carried out by the Jewish National Fund, which specialized in afforestation and land reclamation, the government, in road making, etc., and private employers, who were subsidized to encourage them to "make work." Although the projects were often artificial from the purely economic point of view, they provided the unskilled with opportunities to earn an income and accustomed them to manual labor. In each *ma'barah* there were social workers to handle the individual problems of the immigrants: from the repair of leaking huts and contact with the labor exchange to the running of the local kindergarten and school, the provision of facilities for learning Hebrew, maintenance of sanitary conditions, and full medical and social welfare services. Ninety clinics were established in the *ma'barot*, employing more than 100 doctors and 300 nurses.

Meanwhile, there had been an enormous advance in the establishment of new villages: kibbutzim, mainly manned by young people who had been denied the opportunity to settle on their own because of the White Paper restrictions and the shortage of land, and moshavim, the form favored by the great majority of the newcomers. In 4½ years, up to the end of 1953, 345 new villages—251 moshavim and 96 kibbutzim—with a population of over 20,000 families, were founded—more than in the preceding 70 years. The new settlers cultivated 1,048,000 dunams (262,000 acres) of land, of which 130,000 dunams were irrigated and 53,000 were planted with orchards and vineyards. Their livestock consisted of 660,000 poultry, 22,000 sheep, and 21,000 head of cattle, including 8,000 milch cows. With the aid of Jewish Agency instructors in each village, the apprentice farmers were rapidly increasing their skills, expanding production, and beginning to make a significant contribution to the replacement of imports by home-grown food.

Lull in Immigration. Following the peak, a regression set in: in the years 1952–54 the total number of immigrants was only 51,463. The main reason was the economic recession, which compelled the government to impose a strict austerity regime and reduced the standard of living of the greater part of the population. There was mass unemployment and housing conditions for the immigrants were woefully inadequate. In addition, there was a significant increase in emigration: veteran Israelis and new immigrants were tempted to emigrate to affluent countries, and at times the number who left was higher than the total of those who came in. The lull was used to overhaul the machinery and methods of immigration and absorption. Instead of sending the new arrivals to *ma'barot* or camps, they were taken direct from the ships to homes ready for them and in a few

Table 3. Immigration, 1948–72

Year	Immigrants[1]	Tourists Settling[2]	Temporary Residents[3]	Returning Residents	Total
May 15—Dec. 31, 1948	101,819	9			101,828
1949	239,076	502			239,578
1950	169,405	808			170,213
1951	173,901	1,228			175,129
1952	23,375	994			24,369
1953	10,347	979			11,326
1954	17,471	899			18,370
1955	36,303	1,175			37,478
1956	54,925	1,309			56,234
1957	71,100	1,491			72,591
1958	26,093	1,163			27,256
1959	23,045	908			23,953
1960	23,643	1,023			24,666
1961	46,650	1,067			47,717
1962	59,600	1,855			61,455
1963	62,156	2,278	2,031		66,465
1964	52,456	2,523	1,867		56,846
1965	28,795	2,235	2,068		33,098
1966	13,610	2,348	2,552		18,510
1967	12,275	2,194	3,587	393	18,449
1968	18,156	2,547	8,404	1,964	31,071
1969	23,207	2,260	12,628	2,374	40,469
1970	22,470		15,460	4,111	42,041
1971	25,578		15,660	—	41,238
1972	55,888				55,888
Total	1,391,344	31,795	64,257	8,842	1,496,238

[1] Until 1956 Jews only. [2] Until 1965 Jews only. [3] Figures for temporary residents arriving before 1963 are not available.

days they were able to go out to work. A start was made with the establishment of new "development" towns, some with the *ma'barot* in the Negev and Galilee as nuclei. Thus Yeroḥam was originally a *ma'barah;* the Bet She'arim *ma'barah* became the town of Migdal ha-Emek; and the one at Ḥalsa became Kiryat Shemonah. Other towns were established from the start on a permanent basis, e.g., Dimonah, Kiryat Gat, and Beth-Shemesh, while existing towns, like Afulah and Safed, were given "development" status.

New Methods of Absorption. In 1955 mass immigration was renewed and from 1955 to the end of 1957 most of the immigrants came from Morocco, Tunisia, and Poland. During these years immigration totaled 162,308, as against 51,463 during the slack period of 1952–54. Immigration from Morocco was stimulated by the surge of nationalism which swept that country in 1954 and was further intensified after it achieved independence in March 1956: during these three years 70,053 Moroccan Jews arrived. Following a similar surge of nationalism and the achievement of independence by Tunisia in 1956, 15,267 Jews came from that country during the same period. The political situation in Poland, and particularly the influx of Polish Jews and their families expatriated from the U.S.S.R., also led to a considerable rise in Jewish emigration: 34,426 in the years 1955–57. Following the Hungarian revolution in 1956, thousands of Jews succeeded in fleeing to Austria, whence the Jewish Agency brought over 8,682, and after the Sinai Campaign in the same year 14,562 Egyptian Jews reached Israel.

The absorption of immigrants during this period was facilitated by the country's economic recovery. There was a considerable growth in industry and agriculture and new development projects increased absorptive capacity. The ship-to-settlement method was put into general use; immigrants founded villages and towns in the regional settlement areas, like the Lachish area, in the south, with its central town of Kiryat Gat, and the Taanach area, in the Jezreel Valley, where Afulah was the urban center.

From 1958 to 1960 immigration slowed down again: the total during this period was 72,781. The largest group came from Rumania (27,697) and the total from Eastern Europe was 41,702. During these years there was an increase in the number of professional men among the immigrants: doctors, engineers, economists, and teachers—a trend which had started in 1956. In order to cope with immigrants of this type, the Jewish Agency set up a network of hostels where they could stay with their families in small flats for periods of up to six months, while learning Hebrew and looking for suitable work and housing.

The ulpanim, run jointly with the Ministry of Education and Culture, which was responsible for the teaching, were expanded. Besides the resident ulpanim, which had boarding facilities, there were non-resident ulpanim in the cities, which also catered to part-time students and provided evening classes. Ulpanim were also held in the kibbutzim, where the immigrants put in half a day's work and studied half a day. These schools were described in a UNESCO report as an "excellent institution for adult education." In addition, hundreds of Hebrew courses were run by municipal authorities and voluntary organizations.

After the 1958–60 lull, immigration swelled again from 1961 to 1964, when a total of 215,056 immigrants arrived. There was great disappointment, however, in 1961 and 1962, when most of the 130,000 Algerian Jews who were French citizens, rooted in French civilization, and wished to benefit from the generous assistance given by the French government, opted against *aliyah* when Algeria achieved independence. The great majority settled in France; only 7,700 came to Israel.

During this period the liquidation of the *ma'barot* was speeded up, as more permanent housing schemes were started in all parts of the country. By the end of 1964 only 2,350 families and 980 single persons remained in them; ultimately, only a few who refused to be transferred to permanent homes were left.

Another important factor in the absorption of immigrants was Youth Aliyah (see chapter 7), which took care of their children and sometimes organized their immigration to Ereẓ Israel in advance of their parents.

Educational and Youth Work. The Zionist Organization's educational work among youth and adults in the Diaspora was of considerable long-term importance for *aliyah,* especially from Western Europe and the Americas. The Youth and He-Ḥalutz (Pioneering) Department maintained contact with Zionist and, later, other Jewish movements in the Diaspora (as well as the pioneering youth movements in Israel), providing them with emissaries, guidance, educational material, training facilities, and financial support. Its Institute for Youth Leaders from Abroad in Jerusalem, established in 1946, offered a year of study and work, including five months' study of Hebrew language and literature, Judaism, geography of Israel, the history of Zionism and of Jewish settlement in the Land of Israel, and youth leadership methods, and five months' work and continued study at kibbutzim. In addition, thousands of young people attended the department's annual six- to eight-week Summer and Winter Institutes in Israel. Two departments were set up for education and culture in the Diaspora, one general and one for Torah education and culture. They organized short seminars for teachers in Israel and abroad and set up two permanent centers in Jerusalem for the training of Diaspora teachers: the Ḥayim Greenberg Institute in 1955 and the Rabbi Ze'ev Gold Institute, for religious teachers, in 1957. These and other schemes helped to foster closer links between Israel and the Diaspora, disseminate knowledge of Judaism, strengthen commitment to Israel and the

Western Immigration. The overwhelming majority of the immigrants in the mass-immigration period came from what have been called "lands of stress," and were motivated not only by the positive pull of the free, sovereign Jewish State, but also by the push of various negative factors. Such were the survivors of the Holocaust who wished to have nothing more to do with Europe, the Jews in certain

Table 4. Immigrants by Countries of Origin, May 15, 1948 – Dec. 31, 1972

Country	Number	Country	Number
Eastern Europe	557,858	Africa	397,562
Bulgaria	48,660	Algeria	13,135
Russia	65,882	South Africa	8,097
Yugoslavia	8,092	Tunisia	46,885
Poland	156,195	Libya	34,347
Others	279,029	Morocco	255,633
		Egypt	37,922
Western Europe	85,929	Others	1,543
Italy	4,131	America	98,383
United Kingdom	16,417		
Belgium	3,915	U.S.	47,167
Germany	11,922	Canada	5,281
Holland	4,051	Argentina	24,669
France	31,932	Brazil	6,635
Switzerland	2,192	Mexico	1,586
Spain	660	Chile	3,805
Others	10,709	Uruguay	3,709
		Unregistered	5,531
Asia	331,668		
		Oceania	3,186
India	21,645		
Iran	63,077	Unregistered	22,342
Turkey	56,463		
Others	190,483	All Countries	1,496,928

countries where the defeat of Nazism had failed to stamp out traditional, endemic anti-Semitism, and the Jews in the Arab and Muslim countries. By the early 1970s, in addition to the some three million Jews of Soviet Russia, from which there had never been more than a small trickle of Jewish immigration for family reunion, only about a quarter of a million Jews remained in the "lands of stress."

From 1965 to 1967 there was a decline in the rate of immigration: in 1965 the total fell to 33,098; in 1966 there were only 18,510, and in 1967, 18,065. Many came from Latin America at that period. A number of these people found it hard to settle, in view of the economic recession and other causes, and went back. The Jewish Agency devoted much thought and resources to the requirements of "free" immigration—that is, the immigration of Jews who are free to leave, if they wish, and settle in Israel out of positive motives. The small numbers who came from the "lands of stress" during this period also required, and received, individual treatment.

A first step in this direction was taken in 1965, when the Agency started setting up hostels—actually small-scale hotels—where newcomers could stay for six months, or even a year, while they studied Hebrew at special ulpanim, looked for jobs, decided where they wanted to live, explored possibilities, and became familiar with the conditions of life. Now more of these hostels were set up and the existing ones improved and enlarged. Then the concept was broadened and "absorption centers" were established, each containing all the services and facilities—residential, social, and cultural—that the new immigrants required until they could move into permanent housing. Special personnel helped them to adjust to the new environment, choose schools, and find employment and housing.

To encourage immigration from the free countries it was necessary not only to "process" immigration, but also to further the idea of *aliyah* and encourage prospective immigrants by facilitating their absorption. This kind of immigration was marked by its individualistic character. Each immigrant was moved to *aliyah* by his own reasons and each had his specific potentialities and needs. In addition to his positive inner motivations, he also had to know that he could find in Israel a job in keeping with his training and experience, housing that reasonably approximated what he was used to, and suitable schooling for his children. Immigrants of this type were easily discouraged by bureaucratic inefficiency and the need to make the rounds of Agency and government offices. Those who gave up the struggle and went back deterred others from making the attempt. Most newcomers from the West came in the first place as "temporary residents," changing their status to that of immigrants only when they were assured of successful integration. The government and the Jewish Agency, therefore, had to make special efforts to provide suitable facilities and minimize the "run-around" to which the immigrants objected. Various schemes were initiated by groups of immigrants who set up housing estates in Israel with the Agency's assistance. Some of these were organized by ḥasidic rabbis who lived in the United States and wished to transplant their communities to Israel. The first, Kiryat Tsanz, near Netanyah, was the blueprint for similar projects in other parts of the country.

After the Six-Day War. A significant breakthrough in immigration from the West came after the Six-Day War in 1967. The unprecedented rallying of material and moral support for Israel during the crisis embraced many Jews in the Diaspora who had long since renounced any interest in and concern for things Jewish. It had a particularly cathartic effect on Jewish youth, and over five thousand volunteers went to Israel during May–June 1967 to help in any way they could. By the beginning of 1968, the total number of volunteers from abroad was 7,500, of whom 4,500 went for short periods of up to four months and the rest for six months to a year. They hailed from 40 countries, mainly from Britain (1,900), Latin America (1,500), South Africa (850), France (800), the United States (750), Canada (300), and Australia and New Zealand (275).

More than 4,700 worked in kibbutzim; 450 in moshavim; 1,200 as civilian auxiliaries attached to the Israel Defense Forces; more than 200 in the reconstruction of the University and Hadassah Hospital buildings on Mount Scopus in Jerusalem, and 150 in archaeological excavations; others worked in their own professions, including 225 doctors and nurses, and 100 teachers, youth-group leaders, and social workers, or in land reclamation. The majority received instruction in Hebrew.

About 1,800 remained—as students, or working in their professions or in kibbutzim with a view to permanent settlement. From 1968 volunteers came at a steady annual rate of about 1,800 under various schemes. The largest was Sherut la-Am ("Service to the People")—a year's voluntary service in kibbutzim and development areas. It was estimated that about a third of the volunteers remained in Israel after their year's service, while many of the others eventually returned as immigrants.

There was also a considerable overall increase in *aliyah* from Western countries. On July 10, 1967, the Israel government and the Executive of the Zionist Organization and the Jewish Agency issued a "Call to Aliyah" appealing to the Jewish people the world over to come to Israel and build the land. During the second half of 1967 there was a visible rise in the rate of immigration; in 1968 the total increased to over 30,000, in each of the years 1969, 1970 and 1971 to over 40,000 and in 1972 to an estimated 55,000. To cope with the new mood and the new absorption requirements it was necessary to introduce radical changes in the immigration machinery. Thus in 1967, the three Agency departments involved—Immigration, Absorption, and Economic—were merged into one and a joint Government-Agency Authority on Immigration and Absorption was set up to centralize planning and execution of policy. The Authority worked out various proposals, later passed into law, for special facilities for new immigrants in the spheres of customs, taxation, housing, school and university tuition fees, etc. New absorption centers, hostels, and kibbutz ulpanim were set up all over the country. At the end of 1972 the absorption centers had a capacity of 7,300 beds; hostels, 3,000 beds; students' hostels, 1,400; and kibbutz ulpanim 9,700; and hostels for old people, 700. Since these facilities were intended for half-yearly periods, their annual capacity was double these figures.

In June 1968 the 27th Zionist Congress in Jerusalem decided to found the Aliyah Movement, organized in local circles or countrywide movements in the Diaspora. Each

New immigrants from Latin America arriving at Haifa on the S.S. *Theodor Herzl,* March 1969. Courtesy Government Press Office, Tel Aviv.

member committed himself to settle in Israel within three
 years of joining, but many came within a short period and the

membership was in constant flux, members leaving for *aliyah* and others taking their places. In May 1970 there were 160 *aliyah* circles in 22 countries with a total membership of over 13,000, the largest being in the United States (about 4,000), France (2,700), Argentina (2,100), South Africa (580), Britain (700), and Brazil (600).

With the rapid increase in immigration from the West, absorption became an issue that more directly involved several government agencies, in housing, employment, and other services. It was therefore decided in 1968 to set up a Ministry of Immigrant Absorption. It was agreed that, in the main, the Agency should handle immigration while the Ministry would deal with absorption, but the Agency also continued to be directly responsible for the absorption of needy immigrants and refugees, and operated the hostels, absorption centers, and ulpanim. The work was coordinated by the Authority, whose joint chairmen were the minister of immigrant absorption and the chairman of the Agency

Recent arrivals from the U.S. at the Mevasseret Yerushalayim absorption center, September 1970. Courtesy Government Press Office, Tel Aviv.

Executive, with a coordinating committee meeting once a week. One of the objects of the new arrangements was to cut down on the bureaucratic procedures of absorption which had often come under criticism, especially by newcomers from the West.

The facilities and concessions available to immigrants included: interest-free loans to cover passage and part of shipping costs; exemption from customs and purchase tax on personal and household effects and factory or farm equipment; exemption from purchase tax and reduction in customs on automobiles; exemption from registration fees and part of property tax on purchasing house or business premises; preferential treatment in obtaining employment; partial exemption from income tax and capital gains tax; the right to hold foreign currency for ten years and to redeem State of Israel bonds; accommodation in absorption centers, hostels, and ulpanim; housing on easy terms or assistance in purchase or renting of housing; loans for establishment of businesses; free health assistance through a sick fund for six months; various concessions in national insurance benefits; free secondary schooling and university education; exemption from travel tax. Most of the concessions were available for three years from the date of immigration and also applied to temporary residents.

The government and the Agency established a Student Authority to assist the greatly increased number of students—many of them originally volunteers—who wanted to study in Israel after the Six-Day War. During the academic year 1969/70 there were 7,000 students and 1,500 yeshivah students from abroad in Israel. Over 5,000 of them, who came as immigrants or intended to settle, received assistance and services from the authority: guidance, grants, Hebrew study in ulpanim and support for special preparatory courses. It also helped the universities build additional dormitories and lecture rooms.

Aliyah from the Soviet Union. The Six-Day War was also followed by the intensification of Jewish consciousness and devotion to Israel among Soviet Jews—partly,

Table 5. Immigration of Members of the Professions, 1971

Engineers and surveyors	1,454
Natural sciences	400
Humanities and social sciences	719
Doctors	622
Nurses and midwives	433
Chemists and medical services	315
Teachers and counsellors	1,281
Religious services	124
Lawyers	159
Artists and writers	682
	6,189

Table 6. Immigrants By Age-Group, percentages

	1970[1]	1971
0–14	18.5	21.8
15–19	10.3	10.9
20–29	26.7	22.7
30–44	17.2	17.2
45–64	18.1	18.5
65+	9.2	8.9
	100.0	100.0

[1] Revised figures

it seems, as a reaction against official support for Arab hostility to Israel, and partly due to renewed pride in Israel's achievements. In previous years a few Jews had been allowed to leave the U.S.S.R. to join relatives in Israel, but the Knesset, the government of Israel, and representative Jewish institutions everywhere had always demanded that all Jews who wished to leave the Soviet Union and settle in Israel be permitted to do so.

In 1969 and 1970 there was a new development: scores of Soviet Jews publicly declared, in letters to the Israel

Nathan Tserulnikov from Leningrad (holding flowers), Israel's three millionth citizen, arriving at Lydda airport, January 11, 1971. Walking next to him is Minister of Absorption Nathan Peled. Courtesy Government Press Office, Tel Aviv.

government and international organs signed with full names and addresses, that they regarded Israel as their historic homeland and demanded recognition of the right to *aliyah*, invoking the Declaration on Human Rights which explicitly guarantees the right of every man to leave any country, including his own. Those who were allowed to leave—often after years of effort—reported that there was a widespread awakening among the younger generation, many of whom were studying Hebrew and hoping to come to Israel.

Toward the end of 1970 the severe sentences imposed, after a trial in Leningrad, on a number of Jews accused of planning to hijack a Soviet plane aroused intense indignation among Jews everywhere and widespread support for the Soviet Jews' right to settle in Israel. However, they were not deterred by the trial, the arbitrary bureaucratic obstacles imposed by the authorities, the high charges for permission to leave, and the dismissal of applicants for exit permits, many of whom were thus reduced to destitution while awaiting their visas. Jews continued to demand the recognition of the right to leave, holding public demonstrations and sending delegations to the authorities. Some Jews declared their desire to give up their Soviet citizenship and on May 17, 1971, the Knesset passed a bill enabling the Minister of Interior to grant Israel citizenship to a Jew abroad who has expressed his desire to settle in Israel.

The Soviet authorities began to give way to this pressure. In 1970 only about a thousand Jews were allowed to leave the U.S.S.R.; in 1971 the number rose to 14,500 and in 1972 to about 30,000—an unprecedented figure in the history of *aliyah* from Russia and more than half the total immigration to Israel during the year. About one-third of the total came from the non-Ashkenazi communities of Soviet Georgia and Bukhara; the rest from European U.S.S.R. Another 100,000, approximately, had applied for permission to leave. The *olim* were taken, in the first place, to Vienna, where temporary accommodation was provided, and from there to Israel. The newcomers from the U.S.S.R. included a high proportion of distinguished academics, professional men and technicians, who made a valuable contribution to the Israel economy. However, the integration of the Georgian Jews, who had been accustomed to live in closely-knit, intensely religious communities, and many of whom spoke no language but Georgian, presented special problems. They objected to being dispersed in small groups and arrangements were made to settle them in larger concentrations, in which they could have their own synagogues and continue their characteristic communal life while adapting to the conditions of life in Israel.

In 1972, great indignation was aroused, not only in Israel and throughout the Diaspora, but in many parts of the free world, by the imposition of a crippling exit tax on university and college graduates to compensate the State for the cost of their higher education. After widespread protests, some *olim* were allowed to leave without paying the tax, but it was generally enforced at the end of the year.

There was a melancholy last act to the tragedy of Polish Jewry. After the Six-Day War the Polish government unleashed an anti-Semitic campaign against the small Jewish community that still remained, but allowed them to leave. Of the 20,000 Jews who lived in Poland, about 11,500 left by May 1970, but only 3,500 of them went to Israel.

6 LAW OF RETURN

The Law of Return was passed by the Israel parliament (Knesset) on July 5, 1950, the anniversary of the death of Theodor Herzl. The Law of Return is one of the earliest and most significant of the basic laws of the State of Israel. Declaring that every Jew has the right to settle in Israel as an *oleh* (defined as "a Jew immigrating to Israel for settlement"), it gives legislative confirmation to the age-old Jewish yearning for return to Zion, previously embodied in the Basle Program[17] (1897), in Article 6 of the Mandate for Palestine (1922), and in Israel's Declaration of Independence of May 14, 1948. The law actually sanctioned the existing situation, for, as the official explanatory note pointed out, the Israel Provisional Council of State had, in its first legislative act (the Law and Administration Ordinance, 1948), abolished all restrictions on Jewish immigration and retroactively validated the immigration of every Jew who had, at any time, entered the country—even in contravention of the Mandatory regulations. In the words of the then prime minister, David Ben-Gurion, in presenting the bill to the Knesset for first reading:

> This law lays down not that the State accords the right of settlement to Jews abroad but that this right is inherent in every Jew by virtue of his being a Jew if it but be his will to take part in settling the land. This right preceded the State of Israel, it is that which built the State.

The main provision of the law (section 1), as passed by the Knesset, is accordingly declaratory in nature: "Every Jew has the right to come to this country as an *oleh*." In

[17]Statement of Zionist objectives adopted at First Zionist Congress at Basle in 1897

keeping with the purposes of the law, this status of *oleh* is also accorded to all Jews who had entered the country as immigrants before the law came into force and to all Jews born in the country, whether before or after the law's coming into force (section 4), as well as to any Jew who goes to Israel other than as an immigrant and subsequently expresses his desire to stay and settle in Israel (section 3(a)).

Denial of Oleh's Visa. An *oleh*'s visa may be denied only in cases in which the minister of immigration (later the minister of the interior) is satisfied that the applicant is engaged in activity directed against the Jewish people or is likely to endanger the public health or the security of the State (section 2 (b)). However, a person may not be regarded, for the purpose of this restriction, as endangering the public health on account of an illness contracted after his arrival in Israel (section 3 (b)). Experience indicated that there was another category of persons to whom it was not desirable to give an unrestricted right to settle in Israel as *olim,* namely, wanted criminals who took refuge in Israel or those who intended to continue a life of crime there. The Knesset hesitated to restrict the absolute right of every Jew to *aliyah* and was conscious of the possibilities of rehabilitation of wayward Jews inherent in Israel society. Nevertheless, on Aug. 23, 1954, it adopted an amendment to the law, empowering the minister of the interior to withhold an *oleh*'s visa from "a person with a criminal past, likely to endanger the public welfare" (Law of Return (Amendment) 1954).

The Law of Return further provided the principal method of acquiring Israel nationality, for the Nationality Law, 1952, prescribes that (with certain exceptions) every *oleh* under the Law of Return shall be an Israel national (section 2 (a)).

Legal Problems. The provisions of the law have given rise to a number of legal problems that have come under review by the Israel Courts, in particular the definition of "Who is a Jew?" for the purposes of law. Does the definition of the *halakhah* (Jewish religious law) apply, as in cases of personal status, namely, whoever is born of a Jewish mother or has been duly converted to Judaism; or does the term include any person who bona fide declares himself to be a Jew? In the leading case of *Rufeisen v. Minister of the Interior* ((1962) 17 *P.D.* 2428), the Supreme Court adopted neither of these definitions. It held that, as the Law of Return is a secular enactment, "a Jew" is to be interpreted as Jews in general ordinarily understand it. The court accordingly decided that the law did not apply to a person who, although born a Jew, had subsequently converted to Christianity.

The courts have also been occupied more than once with the question of "criminal past" under section 2 (b) (3) of the law as amended in 1954. In the case of *Jonavici v. Minister of the Interior* ((1958) 33 *P.E.* 415), the court held that, where the minister has reached the conclusion, on the basis of proof, that a criminal past exists, the question whether such past is likely to endanger the public welfare is one for the minister's discretion. Further, a person may have a criminal past though convicted only once, depending on the seriousness of the offense. It has also been decided that "having a criminal past" is not necessarily synonymous with having previous criminal convictions, though it cannot be proved without some substantial evidence of a criminal act previously committed by the applicant: *Gold v. Minister of the Interior* ((1962) 17 *P.D.* 1846); *Lansky v. Minister of the Interior* ((1972) 26 *P.D.* 337).

The Supreme Court was much occupied between 1968 and 1970, in *Shalit's Case* ((1970) 23 *P.D.* (II) 477), with the problem of the status of infant children born in Israel of a Jewish father and a non-Jewish mother. In a controversial decision the Supreme Court, unprecedentedly composed of nine of its ten members, held by a majority of five against four that, since the registration of the particulars prescribed to be notified under the Registration of the Population Law is not evidence of the correctness of such particulars but is, rather, of a statistical character, the registration officer is in duty bound to register them as notified and requested by the person required by law to furnish them.

In the wake of the political controversy aroused by the Shalit decision and upon the initiative of religious circles in the country, the government decided to propose amending legislation so as to clarify that, for the purposes of civil registration and of status under the Law of Return, a Jew is a person born of a Jewish mother or converted to Judaism. The provisions of this bill, as presented to the Knesset and still more as finally adopted, ranged, however, beyond this salient provision, in order to meet the demands of secular circles that the non-Jewish partners, children, or grandchildren of Jewish *olim* should not suffer differential treatment in respect of material rights and privileges accorded to such "*olim,*" including rights under the Nationality Law (Law of Return (amendment no. 2), 5730–1970, enacted in March 1970). These provisions do not extend to a person who, being a Jew, has voluntarily adopted another faith. Likewise, the limitations and conditions applying to a Jew or an *oleh* under the Law of Return or any other relevant enactment apply equally to any person claiming the immigrant rights above referred to. This legislation omits any substantive definition of the concept of conversion to Judaism, and it is accordingly contended that the law does not prescribe a conversion satisfying halakhic requirements.

7 YOUTH ALIYAH

Youth Aliyah was founded for the purpose of rescuing Jewish children and young people from hardship, persecution, or deprivation and giving them care and education in Ereẓ Israel. It started its activities in Germany on the eve of the Nazis' rise to power and saved many children who had to leave their families or were orphaned by the Holocaust. It extended its work to other countries when the need arose and, particularly after the establishment of the State of Israel, looked after many young people entrusted to its care by new immigrant parents already in the country. It developed its own methods for bringing up young people in youth communities in kibbutzim or in its own centers and children's villages. Between the start of the movement in 1933 and the end of 1971, Youth Aliyah cared for over 140,000 young people, of whom 128,000 received residential care: 44% from Europe and the Americas, 41% from Asia and North Africa, and 15% from families already in Israel.

In 1932 Recha Freier, a rabbi's wife in Berlin, conceived the idea of taking Jewish young people doomed to idleness in Germany and bringing them up in Palestine. She contacted the Histadrut, which proposed absorbing them in kibbutzim. The first group of 12 young people was sent out in October 1932 to the Ben Shemen youth village, and on January 30, 1933, the day Hitler became chancellor, the Juedische Jugendhilfe organization was founded, with the cooperation of Jewish youth movements in Germany, to carry on the work.

In the same year the 18th Zionist Congress in Prague decided on the establishment of a department for the settlement of German Jews and the leadership of the department's Youth Aliyah office was entrusted to Henrietta Szold, with the assistance, in matters of finance, of Georg Landauer. In February 1934 the first large group of young people, numbering 60, arrived at the kibbutz En-Harod. A few months later the first religious group was sent to Kevuẓat Rodges, near Petaḥ Tikvah. By the middle of 1935, 600 had been accommodated in 11 kibbutzim, four agricultural schools, and two vocational training centers. In 1935 Hans Beyth, a youth movement leader, became Henrietta Szold's chief assistant and at the end of the year Hadassah undertook the responsibility for financial support of Youth Aliyah. After the Nazi conquest of Austria and Czechoslovakia its work was extended to cover these countries. The need for the rescue of Jewish children from Europe became even more obvious and urgent after the burning of the synagogues and the drastic anti-Jewish measures in Germany in November 1938. By the outbreak of World War II over 5,000 had been brought to Palestine—two-thirds from Germany, one-fifth from Austria and the rest from other countries. For lack of immigration certificates, another 15,000 were sent to Western European countries, especially Britain.

In the early years of World War II (1940–42) it was almost impossible to bring children from Europe and in 1941 Youth Aliyah began to undertake the care of young people already in Palestine. In the same year the first children arrived from oriental countries (mainly Syria), about 1,000 of them crossing the Palestine frontier illegally. In 1943, 800 children from Poland, who had reached Persia via the Soviet Union and were accommodated in a refugee camp in Teheran, were taken to Palestine. There was a heated controversy in the *yishuv* over the education of these children, most of whom were orphans, religious circles demanding that they be given a specifically religious upbringing. The Jewish Agency finally ruled that those over 14 should choose for themselves and younger children should be brought up according to the way of life of their parents.

After the war, soldiers of the Jewish Brigade and emissaries from Ereẓ Israel sought out children in Europe and collected them in transit centers set up by Youth Aliyah, the American Jewish Joint Distribution Committee, O.S.E., and local organizations. Between 1945 and 1948, Youth Aliyah brought over to Palestine about 15,000 children from Europe, mostly survivors of the Holocaust. Many of them arrived illegally and were deported by the British authorities to camps in Cyprus, where a youth village, an imaginative institution which prepared thousands of young people for life in Israel, was established at the beginning of 1947.

With the establishment of the State (1948), Youth Aliyah opened wide its doors to child immigration and care. Its leadership passed to Moshe Kol, who held the post until 1966, when he joined the Israel government and was succeeded by Yizhak Artzi. In 1968 the post was entrusted to Yosef Klarman. Between 1948 and the end of 1971, 97,382 young people passed through its hands—about 52% of them coming from Asian and North African countries, 31% from Europe and the Americas, and 17% from Israel (mostly of African and Asian origin).

Religious youth are brought up in youth villages and institutions, including yeshivot, and in religious kibbutzim, belonging to all trends in religious Jewry. Forty per cent of Youth Aliyah wards are accommodated in religious centers. In 1958 Youth Aliyah was awarded the Israel Prize in education for its humanitarian, social, and educational achievements.

Educational Methods. Successive waves of immigration brought in very varied types of children, differing widely in origin, previous education, and social, economic, and cultural background, many of whom had undergone traumatic experiences before their arrival. Youth Aliyah's aim, moreover, was not merely instruction and physical welfare, but education in the widest sense of the term in order to enable the child to find his place and play his part in a new and dynamic society. It was necessary, therefore, to develop new

Table 7. Youth Accepted for Training from the Outset of Youth Aliyah to Jan. 1, 1970 (by countries of origin)

Country of Origin	19 Feb. 34 1 Oct. 39	1 Oct. 39 1 Oct. 45	1 Oct. 45 1 Oct. 48	1 Oct. 48 1 Jan. 72	19 Feb. 34 1 Jan. 72
Rumania	29	1,736	5,141	9,542	16,448
Poland	139	1,401	3,813	3,722	9,075
Germany	3,437	1,454	255	814	5,960
Israel	–	1,123	922	16,722	18,767
Morocco	–	1	34	19,152	19,187
Iraq	–	73	190	6,937	7,200
Turkey	–	1,045	64	4,228	5,397
Bulgaria	–	457	686	2,552	3,695
Hungary	–	395	1,333	1,928	3,656
Yemen	–	380	154	4,062	4,596
Czechoslovakia	354	530	647	1,010	2,541
Austria	997	634	69	148	1,848
Iran	–	3	9	4,398	4,410
Algeria and Tunisia	–	1	30	3,675	3,706
Egypt	–	6	69	2,230	2,305
Syria and Lebanon	–	214	234	909	1,357

Benelux	–	131	190	535	856
Libya	–	24	23	1,028	1,075
France	–	103	85	1,203	1,391
Yugoslavia	–	108	34	509	651
India	–	–	1	2,352	2,353
Greece	–	220	121	121	462
Russia	–	–	107	3,949	4,106
Italy	–	151	32	241	424
Other European countries	–	75	134	515	724
Asia and Africa	–	3	–	966	969
The Americas	–	1	4	3,360	3,365
Total	4,956	10,269	14,381	96,918	126,524
Unspecified	56	886	639	474	2,055
Grand Total	5,012	11,155	15,020	97,382	128,579

educational methods and forms of youth care, a task that demanded acute pedagogical insight and much initiative and innovation. To integrate the children into the social fabric of the new environment and at the same time give them individual attention, Youth Aliyah utilized two distinctive instruments: the *ḥevrat no'ar* (youth community) and the *madrikh* ("guide," counsellor, or youth leader).

The *ḥevrat no'ar* became the characteristic educational unit of Youth Aliyah. It comprised about 40 young people who stayed together for two to four years until the age of 17–18 and constituted a self-contained social group with a large measure of internal autonomy. It might be attached to a kibbutz, which thus became an "educational settlement," or be part of a youth village or other educational institution directly managed by Youth Aliyah. The young people generally devoted four hours to work on the farm or in the workshop and four to study, in addition to communal and group activities.

Each *ḥevrat no'ar* had a *madrikh* and a *metappelet* (house mother) who helped the young people to tackle their personal, emotional, educational, and social problems as individuals and as a coherent and self-disciplined group. In the early years most of the *madrikhim* were temporary, coming from the kibbutzim for a spell of duty, but considerable efforts were made to enhance the status and standards of their vocation as a branch of the teaching profession. Seminaries for Youth Aliyah *madrikhim* and teachers were conducted in coordination with the Ministry of Education and Culture, especially its agricultural education division. Many graduates of Youth Aliyah have become *madrikhim*.

From 1949 onward, the proportion of children from African and Asian countries—mostly from underprivileged homes—rose until in 1953 they constituted 80% of the total. After a study of the problems involved in the care and education of these children, Youth Aliyah educators were able to confirm that there were no "ethnic" causes for their apparent backwardness, which was the result of generations of poverty and neglect. Specially graded curricula were devised for these children, textbooks and teaching materials were designed for the purpose, and teachers were given special guidance in this type of work.

At the beginning of the 1970s, Youth Aliyah was an educational, rather than a rescue organization, bringing up young newcomers from developed countries, as well as from areas of distress. Many were accommodated in youth villages, receiving education on the secondary level—vocational, agricultural, or academic—enabling some of them to prepare for matriculation and—if fit—go on to one of the universities. There was a scholarship fund for gifted children. Youth Aliyah's educational system was recognized by the Ministry of Education and Culture and controlled by its own inspectors. At the Ne'urim-Hadassah center, a joint venture of Youth Aliyah and Hadassah, a large variety of special vocational training courses were held. At Ramat Hadassah and Kiryat Ye'arim there were special courses for educationally backward and emotionally disturbed children. There were also medical and child guidance services.

For children in development areas living with their parents (mostly new immigrants), Youth Aliyah has established day centers in new towns and villages, which it runs jointly with the Jewish Agency and the ministries of Labor and Education. In 1970 there were 15 of these centers, giving a full day's vocational training and general education to over 1,000 children aged 14–16 who had failed to gain admission to local post-primary schools or had dropped out before completing the course. There were also advanced one-year courses for graduates of the centers (some of them at Ne'urim). Youth Aliyah *ulpanim* were established for young immigrants aged 16–17½. A late innovation was the establishment of foreign-language courses at which young people from abroad can complete their secondary education in their native language up to matriculation standard and at the same time learn Hebrew and Jewish subjects.

Of the 125,000 children and young people taken in by Youth Aliyah up to the end of 1970 (in addition to some 15,000 in day centers), 9% came from Western Europe, 33% from Eastern Europe, 2% from the Americas, 21% from Africa, 20% from Asia, and 15% from Israel. During the year 1970, 1,351 new wards were received: 29% from Israel, 19% from African countries, 19% from Mediterranean countries, 11% from the Americas, 9% from Eastern Europe, 8% from Western Europe, and 5% from other Asian countries. On Jan. 1, 1971, Youth Aliyah had 7,551 wards under its care: about 70% in its 80 residential institutions, 19% in 150 kibbutz centers, 6% at special courses, and 5% at *ulpanim*. In addition, 1,631 young people attended day centers for youth, making a total of 9,182 under Youth Aliyah's care. Youth Aliyah graduates made up over 10% of Israel's Jewish population between the ages of 15 and 50 (50 being more or less the age of the earliest wards in 1971). They are about 20% of the membership of the kibbutzim and 30% in religious kibbutzim.

Youth Aliyah also found many non-Jewish supporters who were impressed by its work, including personalities like Eleanor Roosevelt, who was its World Patron. It is affiliated to various international organizations and is an active member of the International Federation of Children's Communities (FICE) and the International Union for Child Welfare.

8 SETTLEMENT

Until World War I. Modern Jewish settlement (*hityashevut*) in the Land of Israel is usually reckoned by historians as beginning with the founding of Petaḥ Tikvah in 1878 by Jews from Jerusalem, with the aid of a group from Hungary. The Zionist movement initially left urban resettlement almost entirely to private initiative, so that the term *hityashevut* was identified with the establishment of new villages. It is only in recent years that it has been extended to cover the development of new towns and urban areas.

THE FIRST SETTLEMENTS. The impetus to the large-scale renewal of Jewish settlement on the land was given by the First Aliyah. The newcomers founded Rishon le-Zion, Zikhron Ya'akov, and Rosh Pinnah in 1882, Yesud ha-Ma'alah and Ekron in 1883, Gederah in 1884, and Reḥovot, Mishmar ha-Yarden, and Ḥaderah in 1890. They were primarily interested in setting up agricultural communities and tried to establish villages like those they had known in Europe, calling them moshavot. Many obstacles were placed in the way of the settlers by the Turkish authorities, and few of them had the slightest knowledge of farming methods. It was not long before the moshavot were threatened with collapse.

At this stage Baron Edmond de Rothschild stepped in. He made considerable investments in the farms, sent out experts to teach viticulture, and installed his own administrators. The settlements were saved, but at a considerable price: the settlers became completely dependent on outside support and had little say in the management of their holdings. By 1898 there were 22 of the new Jewish villages in the country, most of them based on monoculture, with

Table 8. Population and Area of the Jewish Settlements in 1898

Region	Settlement	Inhab-itants	Area (in dunams[1])
Judea	Mikveh Israel	225	2,600
	Rishon le-Zion	531	6,800
	Nes Ziyyonah	121	1,800
	Reḥovot	281	10,500
	Ekron	150	4,090
	Gederah	69	3,400
	Be'er Toviyyah	105	5,630
	Moẓa	15	650
	Hartuv	28	5,000
Samaria	Petaḥ Tikvah	502	13,850
	Ḥaderah	870	29,880
	Kefar Sava	153	7,500
	Tanturah and Athlit	1,070	20,000
	Zikhron Ya'akov	—	—
Galilee	Sejerah	—	27,000
	Rosh Pinnah	325	14,000
	Ein Zeitim	51	5,600
	Mishmar ha-Yarden	93	2,380
	Yesud ha-Ma'alah	100	12,500
	Meron	—	2,000
	Maḥanayim	—	8,500
	Metullah	233	12,000

[1] Four dunams = one acre.

fruit plantations as their mainstay. In 1900 the Jewish Colonization Association (ICA, founded in 1891), which at first acted only as a source of credit for the farm communities, took over the management from Rothschild's administration. It developed a wider range of activities, established a training farm for agricultural laborers in Sejerah (1901) and founded Mesḥa (Kefar Tavor), Menaḥemiyyah, and Yavne'el (1902), Beit Gan (1902), and Mizpeh (1908), based on field crops (cereals).

THE ZIONIST ORGANIZATION'S ROLE. In 1898, at the Second Zionist Congress, the Zionist Organization recognized the major role of settlement in the national revival, appointing a committee for the purpose. It started real activity, however, only after the foundation of the Jewish National Fund in 1901 and, in particular, after the establishment of its Palestine Department and Palestine Office, headed by Arthur Ruppin, in 1907 and 1908 respectively. Many of the newcomers of the Second Aliyah wanted to work on the land; at first they sought employment in the existing villages, which employed Arabs almost exclusively, and then, in 1908, began to found their own settlements. The Zionist Organization's first settlement enterprise, in 1908, was the Dalāyikat Umm Jūnī training farm on the Jordan. In the following year the Palestine Office handed over part of the farm at Dalāyika, on the west bank of the river, to a group of seven workers who set up the first kevuẓah or collective village, which they called Kinneret. Another group later leased the land at Umm Jūnī, on the east bank, on similar terms; it was later called Deganyah. A third venture, in Merḥavyah, based on the cooperative principles of Franz Oppenheimer, proved a failure.

Starting with field crops, Deganyah and Kinneret gradually added new types of agriculture. Yosef Bussel, one of the founders of Deganyah, suggested diversified farming, combining fruit plantations with field crops and animal husbandry, so that the kevuẓah could pay its way and lay the foundation for permanent settlement. Ruppin and Y. A. Elazari- Volcani, who was then setting up an agricultural research station at Ben Shemen, supported the idea, which gradually gained general acceptance. Settlement progressed slowly but steadily until the end of World War I, spreading to new areas in which the Jewish National Fund had acquired land. The moshavot also donated plots of land for daughter settlements, which were set up in 1912–13 by immigrants from Yemen: Maḥaneh Yehudah on the outskirts of Petaḥ Tikvah, Naḥali'el near Ḥaderah, and Sha'arayim near Reḥovot, "Workers' neighborhoods" —

Early settlers in the courtyard of Kinneret, in Galilee, 1910. Courtesy Central Zionist Archives, Jerusalem.

auxiliary farms for farm laborers were established in Ein Gannim, Naḥalat Yehudah, and Ein-Hai (Kefar Malal), as well as independent villages like Gan Shemu'el, founded in 1913. By the beginning of World War I there were 47 Jewish villages in the country, 14 of them supported by the Zionist Organization through the Palestine Office.

Under the Mandate. KIBBUTZ AND MOSHAV. During World War I, settlement activities came to a virtual standstill, but in 1919, after the Balfour Declaration and the start of the Third Aliyah, activities were resumed by the Zionist Organization's Settlement Department, which replaced the Palestine Office. Much attention was paid to the ideological, as well as the practical aspects of the work. The ideal of the kevuẓah or kibbutz (the latter term was first used for the large settlement of En-Harod, founded in 1921) was fully defined. In 1920 a renewed attempt was made, on a scientific basis, to settle in the hill areas, with the establishment of Kiryat Anavim, west of Jerusalem, and Atarot, to the north of the city. (Previous attempts had been made at Moẓa, in 1894, and Hartuv, in 1895.) Between 1921 and 1923 four kevuzot and three kibbutzim were founded in the Jezreel Valley—Emek Yizre'el, known simply as the Emek—where the first large, continuous stretches of land for settlement had been purchased by the JNF.

At the same time a new type of settlement—the cooperative smallholders' village or moshav—developed out of the workers' neighborhoods, but while the latter were intended as auxiliary farms for farm laborers working elsewhere, the moshavim were designed for independent settlers. This development, suggested by Eliezer Joffe, was first applied in 1921 at Nahalal, in the Emek.

With the acquisition of additional areas in the Kishon basin, southeast of Haifa, in the Jordan Valley, and on the Coastal Plain, the network expanded. The land remained in the ownership of the JNF, which leased it to the settlers for long terms. The settlements established by the Zionist Organization were based mainly on diversified farming, including fruit plantations, field crops, and livestock. Some private villages, based mainly on citrus, also made headway, and moshavot were founded: Binyaminah in 1922, and Pardes Ḥannah and Ramatayim in 1928, mainly by middle-class settlers who raised all or part of the funds by their own efforts, requiring less help from the Settlement Department.

Standardizing Farm Units. As yet there were no well-defined types of farms. The size of holdings was not standardized, and the various villages engaged in different varieties of mixed agriculture, so that income levels varied greatly. To encourage standardization, the Zionist Executive appointed a committee in 1929 to devise a "farm index" for the different parts of the country. It examined the size of holding required for a family's livelihood, the equipment and supplies needed per unit, and the crops and livestock best suited to each area. In irrigated areas, such as the Beth-Shean and Jordan valleys and the Coastal Plain, 25 dunams ($6\frac{1}{4}$ acres) were allotted for each farm unit; in non-irrigated or partially irrigated areas, such as the Jezreel Valley, 140 to 280 dunams (35–70 acres). This was the first step toward overall agricultural planning based on the natural conditions of the country.

As irrigation was extended, Volcani proposed reducing the farm unit to 24–30 dunams, to be made viable by more intensive methods, so as to facilitate the maximum utilization of the limited land resources and maintain the principle of "personal labor" *(avodah aẓmit)*, to which both moshavim and kibbutzim adhered. The system also enabled each settlement to become an autonomous unit, almost independent of outside supplies and able, if necessary, to subsist in isolation and withstand a state of siege. Volcani's "organic diversified farm" became the prevalent type in Jewish agriculture during the Mandatory period and the early years of statehood.

The countrywide federations of kibbutzim and moshavim, run by the villagers' representatives, played an important role: they recruited new members, made regulations for the affiliated settlements, and dealt with economic problems. Newcomers were frequently organized abroad as "nuclei" *(garinim)*, which could settle as a group immediately on arrival. Sometimes the organizations set up new villages on their own, without initial assistance from the Settlement Department of the Jewish Agency, which took them under its wing at a much later stage.

SPECIAL SETTLEMENT PROJECTS. Between the early 1930s and World War II, a number of special settlement projects were carried out. The "Thousand Family Project" (which in the end comprised only a few hundred families) was started in 1932 and led to the founding of several villages on the Coastal Plain near Reḥovot— Kefar Bilu, Neta'im, Bet Oved—and in the Sharon region— Ẓofit, Kefar Hess, Rishpon, and others. Immigrants from Germany, starting in 1933, set up villages in the Ḥefer Plain and the Sharon. The Arab riots of 1936–39 inspired a new method of setting up outposts overnight: the Stockade and Watchtower *(ḥomah u-migdal)* settlements, in order to forestall Arab attacks and official British opposition. The Zionist Organization decided to speed up the pace of settlement and set up strongpoints in areas, where Jews had not lived previously,

A Jewish settlement in the Ḥefer Valley, c. 1930. Courtesy Central Zionist Archives, Jerusalem.

so as to create a new Jewish population map in case partition was adopted. The main areas concerned were the Beth-Shean Valley and Upper Galilee. In all, 53 new villages, mostly based on diversified farming, were set up between 1936 and 1939. Despite the White Paper restrictions, the establishment of new villages continued during and after World War II: 94 were founded, almost half of them during the war. After the end of hostilities, there was a renewed effort to extend the area of Jewish settlement, special attention being devoted to the northern Negev, where 11 new villages were set up in a single night (Day of Atonement, 1946). Seven more were set up in 1947, and a provisional pipeline was laid from the center of the country to provide them with water.

In the State of Israel. The War of Independence in 1948 provided ample validation of the doctrine that settlement ensures control. Practically all areas in which there were Jewish settlements, however few or isolated, withstood the invading Arab armies and helped to determine the boundaries of the state. Political and economic conditions were completely transformed, and the

Assembling the model for the "tower and stockade" kibbutz of Sha'ar ha-Golan on the day of settlement, May 3, 1938. Courtesy Keren Hayesod, United Israel Appeal, Jerusalem.

new situation led to a new settlement policy, much broader in scope, covering wider areas, and founded on new organizational and economic principles. The severe food shortage of the first few years necessitated an immediate increase in farm production. At the same time employment had to be found for the new immigrants, many of whom lacked vocational training. Land was no longer a problem, since there were large unsettled areas within the armistice boundaries, though they were exposed to marauders.

Vast agricultural settlement projects were launched, with the Jewish Agency's Settlement Department still in charge. The department was responsible for the planning, execution, and supervision of the work, including the siting of the villages; the planning of buildings, water supply, and

Planting the first trees in Ein ha-Shofet, a kibbutz in the Jezreel Valley, 1937. Courtesy Keren Hayesod, United Israel Appeal, Jerusalem.

irrigation networks; the provision of equipment, seeds, and livestock; and expert guidance in farming methods and the problems involved in the establishment of self-reliant, socially integrated rural communities. Veteran farmers were sent to live in the villages as instructors and, in the early stages, help the villagers solve their social problems. At first

Table 9. Jewish Agricultural Settlements and Population up to the Establishment of the State

Year	Moshavot		Moshavim		Kibbutzim		Others[2]		Total	
	Settlements	Inhabitants	Settlements	Inhabitants	Settlements	Inhabitants	Settlements	Inhabitants	Settlements	Inhabitants
End of 1900	21	4,950					1	260	22	5,210
End of 1914	32	11,000	3	400	4	180	8	410	47	11,990
End of 1922	34	11,540	11	1,410	19	1,190	7	780	71	14,920
End of 1941	45	63,240	94	24,820	87	23,190	5	1,750	231	113,000
End of 1944	44	76,000	99	29,500	111	33,500	5	4,000	259	143,000
May 1948	15[1]	24,160	99	30,142	159	54,208	4	2,121	277	110,631

[1] Some rural settlements have become urban. [2] Agricultural schools, farms, etc.

Table 10.
Jewish Agricultural Settlements Founded After the Establishment of the State[1] (Settlement Department, Jewish Agency)

Year	Moshavim and work villages	Kibbutzim	Total number settlements
1948	5	20	25
1949	60	42	102
1950	114	13	127
1951	24	7	31
1952	12	3	15
1953	36	9	45
1954	8	2	10
1955	12	4	16
1956	12	8	20
1957–60	14	4	18
1961–64	2	4	6
1965–67	2	2	4
1968–72	24	22	46
Total	325	140	465

[1] In addition, there are 50 extensions of existing settlements and 22 educational institutions and agricultural farms.

the settlers were employed largely in building or (in the case of abandoned Arab villages) repairing houses, paving roads, and laying pipelines; they were usually provided with outside employment in afforestation and the like until they could live on the produce of their farms. The department's central and regional offices, with their expert agronomists, engineers, and architects, supervised the work of the men in the field and, in conjunction with the Ministry of Agriculture, coordinated the choice of crops and the methods of cultivation in accordance with the climatic and soil conditions in various parts of the country.

In each of the two years 1948/49 and 1950/51, some 100 new settlements were founded, at first mainly in abandoned Arab villages on the Coastal Plain and in the mountains of Jerusalem and Galilee, then in the Negev, the Lachish and

Adullam areas in the south, the Taanach area in the eastern Jezreel Valley, and finally in the arid Arabah. Settlements in border areas were sometimes established first as outposts by Naḥal units of the Israel Defense Forces and some of them later became civilian villages.

Between the end of 1947 (when the U.N. partition resolution was passed) and 1972, 465 new villages were established, with about 28,000 families living in them, while many existing ones were expanded and new urban communities established.

Popularity of the Moshav. An outstanding feature of this period was the growing popularity of the moshav. Before independence kibbutzim outnumbered moshavim; of the new villages founded subsequently (up to the end of 1972), 325 were moshavim and only 140 kibbutzim. The development is shown in Table 10. The main reason for the shift was the ethnic and social background of the newcomers. Before 1948 most of the immigrants who were of European origin intended from the first to become farmers. The later arrivals, on the other hand, over half of whom came from Asia and Africa, were placed on the land without any prior practical or ideological preparation. The collective structure, making as it does much greater ideological demands on the individual, hardly suited their social background and they preferred the moshavim, which are closer to the ordinary type of village.

MODIFICATION OF FARM PATTERNS. Until 1953 most of the new villages were based on diversified farming because of the urgent need for fresh agricultural produce, especially milk, eggs, vegetables, and fruit. The structure of the farms was almost identical with the diversified organic farm type, for which the pattern had been set some 15 years before, and it was only after the beginning of 1953 that certain modifications were introduced. In some of the newly settled regions, the hill areas and the Negev, natural and climatic conditions were not suited to this type of farming. Moreover, production methods had improved and increasing mechanization called for greater specialization. The political conditions which had required small farm units and large settlements crowded into a small space, or autonomous units independent of outside supplies, no longer existed. The diversified farm model was therefore gradually abandoned or modified. Specialized farms were set up according to specific local conditions and domestic and foreign market requirements, the farms in each region now specializing in a particular branch of agriculture. Most of the moshavim established in 1955—in the Lachish region, for instance— were based on field crops, allowing almost twice as much land per farmer as the diversified farms—some 50 dunams ($12\frac{1}{2}$ acres) per unit. Industrial crops for export or for replacement of imports, as well as vegetables for consumption and processing, are grown. Farms suited for growing export vegetables are located in special areas, mainly the Besor region in the western Negev. The diversified farms have also been modified in the direction of greater specialization, most of them being converted into dairy farms, while others concentrate on citrus, vegetables, and similar special products.

REGIONAL SETTLEMENT SCHEMES. The political, economic, and social changes that followed the establishment of the State of Israel have also affected the rural pattern. Instead of each village being a closed, independent economic and social unit, they are integrated in a comprehensive regional structure. A pattern of this kind was first adopted in the Negev settlements founded between 1951 and 1952, which were clustered around service centers, and was further developed in the Lachish area, settled in 1955. The pattern is based on the comprehensive planning of all the agricultural settlements and urban and rural centers in the area. The villages are placed in clusters of four or five around a rural center which provides the necessary facilities, while a larger town community serves the whole region. Only everyday facilities—kindergarten, food store, synagogue, etc.—are situated within the village itself. Other services, such as schools, shopping centers, sorting and packing sheds, and tractor stations, are located in the rural center, while more widely used facilities are located in the regional town. Since larger populations are catered for, the services are cheaper and more efficient, while civil servants, teachers, technicians, and the like can live in the rural center. Industries, mainly processing plants, are sited in the regional towns, closer to supplies of raw materials, thus reducing transportation costs. Services and industries located in the midst of the rural areas provide jobs for the surplus manpower in the villages, stemming the flow to the towns and preventing the impoverishment and abandonment of the countryside.

The regional structure also facilitates greater integration among settlers from different parts of the world, whose divergent backgrounds make it undesirable to make them live in close proximity. Under the regional system each village can be made up of a single ethnic group, while all the groups use the facilities provided at the rural center, where there is contact with people from the other villages. The result is a gradual process of integration which does not disrupt the life of the individual communities. Steps are being taken to establish rural service centers in areas settled before 1954, when the regional system was introduced.

Regional cooperation has also developed among the kibbutzim, which have begun to set up joint ventures. Here, for ideological and social reasons, the service center is not actually lived in; it contains facilities and plants shared by a number of kibbutzim, but does not constitute a separate village, the staff living in adjacent kibbutzim or coming in from a nearby town. A typical example is the center maintained by the Sha'ar ha-Negev regional council, in which 11 kibbutzim jointly run a refrigeration plant, a poultry slaughterhouse and a cotton gin, besides an amphitheater, sports facilities, a regional school, a regional laundry, and other consumer services.

NATIONAL PLANNING. Another direct consequence of statehood is that land settlement has become an integral part of the national physical and economic master plans.
 Under the Mandatory regime, when there was no overall

planning and development, the Jewish Agency's Settlement Department was practically independent. Now settlement is a part of national development, and close coordination is therefore maintained with all the other planning authorities. This considerably facilitates integration of rural and urban development: settlement activities are no longer confined to the rural areas, and every project has to take into account urban developments in the neighborhood. Thus, a development project for the Galilee area, started in 1966, covers the entire region, including, in addition to villages and rural centers, towns like Nazareth, Karmi'el, and Safed. Joint teams representing the Settlement Department and all the other competent authorities collaborate in the preparation of such projects. In line with this trend, the Jewish Agency and the Ministries of Housing, Labor, and Agriculture have set up a Rural and Urban Settlement Study Center to investigate the problems involved and outline suitable methods for new development

Young settlers unloading beds at Naḥal Snir on the Golan Heights, November 1967. Courtesy Government Press Office, Tel Aviv.

and the modification of existing settlement patterns. The new regions now being developed in this way are central Galilee, the Besor Region and the western Negev, and the Arabah.

Since the Six-Day War (until 1972). Agricultural settlement has made an important contribution to the maintenance of security in the areas administered by Israel lines against infiltration and sabotage. Up to 1972, 16 villages and urban or semi-urban centers were established in the Golan Heights, four in Samaria, five in the Gaza Strip and Northern Sinai, and three on the east coast of Sinai. Three villages have been resettled in the Eẓyon area, north of Hebron, where four were destroyed by the Arab Legion. In addition, 10 new villages have been established in the Arabah since the Six-Day War.

9 LAND OWNERSHIP

Under Ottoman Rule. In Palestine until 1858, there were no official title deeds to document ownership of land. There was a plentiful supply for all who wished to cultivate the land, and no one needed to establish official ownership of a specific plot. In the hills, in particular, there were large uncultivated areas, which were used only for spring pasture. In 1858 the Ottoman government promulgated the *ṭābū* law, designed to enforce registration and establish ownership for all land. But the obligation was no more than theoretical: only limited areas were registered, and many holders did not register their lands at all, to facilitate evasion of taxes and other imposts. Many peasants recorded the natural boundaries of their land but deliberately underestimated the area—there was no cadastral survey at the time. In return for a few coppers other peasants waived their rights in favor of *effendis* (rich landlords) in the towns. Lands were sometimes registered in the name of a whole village (*mushā'a* land) without stipulating the names of the current holders; the area was divided up afresh every year according to the number of members in each family, with a steady decrease in the area of the individual holding. Much land was left uncultivated because it had not been manured for centuries and the exhausted soil afforded inadequate yields, while the burden of taxation and extortion by the authorities and the tax farmers was heavy.

The enforcement of the *maḥlūl* law, under which cultivable land untilled for three consecutive years escheated to the state, led to the concentration of considerable areas in the hands of the government, which, being unable

سبب تصدير توقيع همايون اولدركه
دفترخانهٔ خاقانی یه ورود ایدن زیرده نومرو وشهری محرر دفتردن مستبان اولدیغی
وجهله [illegible] سنجاغنده [illegible] قضاسنده [illegible]
[illegible] ایله محدود
تخمینا [illegible] اون سنه دنبرو یدنده سندی اولمیه رق
بلا نزاع ضبط وتصرف ایتمش اولدیغی تبین ایدرك حق قراری ثابت اولغله [illegible] مأموریته
دا ایلك اوزره کماکان تصرفنه اذن ویرلش اولدیغی مشعر اشبو سند اعطا قلندی فی
سنه ١٢٩٠

دفتر شهری

صیره نومروسی
٤٧

Title deed from Ottoman period, 1874. The title, for land near Jerusalem, was granted to an individual following ten years of unchallenged possession. Jerusalem, Hebrew University, Ben-Zvi Institute, Navon Collection.

to cultivate them, leased them to urban capitalists for trivial rents. As a result, extensive stretches were concentrated in the hands of individual rich landowners, the sultan (*Jiftlik* land), the state, and the waqf (Muslim public, state, or religious trust), to which land was often dedicated to avoid taxation. At the end of the 19th century, large estates were owned by the state and the sultan at Beersheba and Beth-Shean and in the Ḥuleh and Jordan valleys; by *effendis* and foreigners in the valley of Jezreel, along the

Leaders of the Warsaw Menuḥah ve-Naḥalah Society, established for buying land in Ereẓ Israel, 1890. Left to right, Eliezer Kaplan, Ze'ev Gluskin, Eliezer Ze'ev Lewin-Epstein, and Mattityahu Cohen. Courtesy Central Zionist Archives, Jerusalem.

coast, and in various villages, and by village communities, charitable institutions and associations.

Jewish land purchases outside the four "holy cities" of Jerusalem, Hebron, Safed, and Tiberias began in 1855 with the acquisition of 100 dunams (25 acres) of citrus groves near Jaffa by Sir Moses Montefiore. This was followed by the purchase of land at Moẓa, near Jerusalem, in 1859, at Mulabbas (Petaḥ Tikvah) in 1878, and ʿUyūn Qārā (Rishon le-Zion), Zammārīn (Zikhron Ya'akov), and Jā'ūna (Rosh Pinnah) in 1882. By the end of 1882, 22,000 dunams (5,500 acres) of land, mostly rural, were in Jewish possession. Jews bought much land after 1882, mainly from owners of large estates, and owned 418,000 dunams (104,500 acres) at the outbreak of World War I.

Under the Mandate. There was no considerable change in land ownership during the war, but, after the Allied occupation and the establishment of British Mandatory rule in 1920, the old Ottoman land registries were reopened and transactions renewed. A special Land Court was established, at first in the north, to expedite determination of ownership on the basis of surveys, documents, and prescriptive rights. With increased Jewish immigration, more land was purchased, still mainly from owners of large estates. By November 1947, when the U.N. decided on the partition of Palestine, Jews had 1,820,000 dunams (455,000 acres) of land, of which 800,000 dunams (200,000 acres) were owned by the Jewish National Fund (J.N.F.), 450,000 by the Palestine Jewish Colonization Association (PICA), and the rest by public and private companies and by individuals.

In Independent Israel. The area of the State of Israel, within the armistice demarcation lines of 1949, was 20,700,000 dunams. Of these 425,000 were covered by water and of the remaining 20,255,000 dunams the state owned 17,675,000 dunams; the J.N.F. 800,000 dunams; PICA 450,000; Jewish individuals 510,000 dunams; and Arab individuals 820,000 dunams. State lands included 14,500,-000 dunams inherited from the Mandatory government

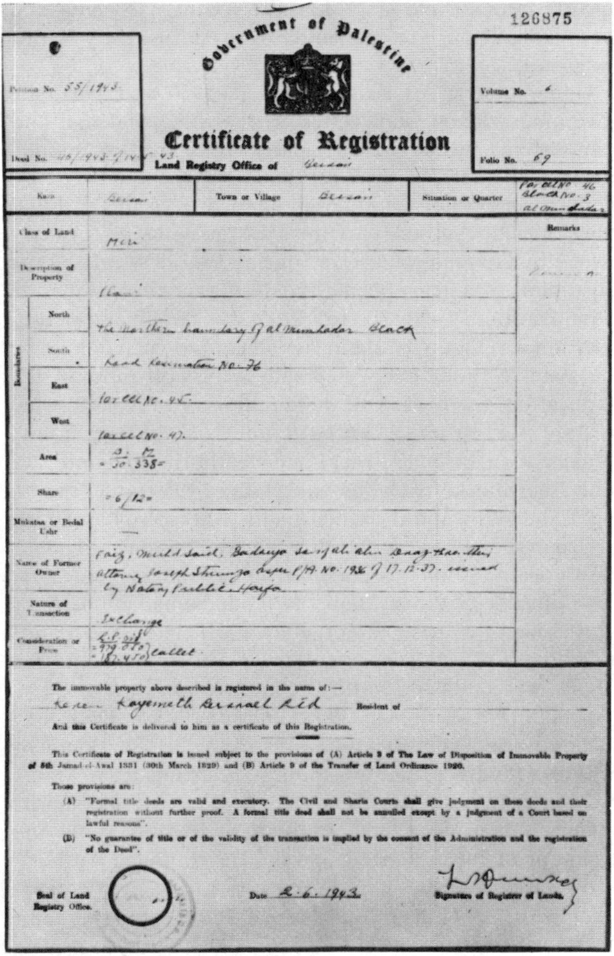
126875

Government of Palestine

Certificate of Registration

Petition No. 55/1943

Deed No. [illegible] 43

Land Registry Office of Beisan

Volume No. 6

Folio No. 69

Kaza	Beisan	Town or Village	Beisan	Situation or Quarter	Parcel No. 46 Block No. 3 al Mundadar

		Remarks
Class of Land	Mulk	
Description of Property		
Boundaries: North	The northern boundary of al Mumhadar Block	
South	Road Reservation No. 76	
East	Parcel No. 45	
West	Parcel No. 47	
Area	D. M = 30. 338 =	
Share	= 6/12 =	
Mukataa or Bedal Ushr	—	
Name of Former Owner	Faiz, Mulhid Said, Badayo Sasaf ali alias Daoud through their attorney Joseph Shemgo as per P/A No. 1936 of 17.12.37 issued by Notary Public Haifa	
Nature of Transaction	Exchange	
Consideration or Price	L.P. 0.18 = 979.080 = 182.450 called	

The immovable property above described is registered in the name of:— Keren Kayemeth Leisrael Ltd Resident of

And this Certificate is delivered to him as a certificate of this Registration.

This Certificate of Registration is issued subject to the provisions of (A) Article 3 of The Law of Disposition of Immovable Property of 5th Jamad-el-Awal 1331 (30th March 1329) and (B) Article 9 of the Transfer of Land Ordinance 1920.

Those provisions are:

(A) "Formal title deeds are valid and executory. The Civil and Sharia Courts shall give judgment on these deeds and their registration without further proof. A formal title deed shall not be annulled except by a judgment of a Court based on lawful reasons".

(B) "No guarantee of title or of the validity of the transaction is implied by the consent of the Administration and the registration of the Deed".

Seal of Land Registry Office.

Date 2.6.1943

Signature of Registrar of Lands.

Registration certificate of the Government of Palestine, issued to the Jewish National Fund in respect of a parcel of land in the Beth-Shean Valley, 1943. Courtesy J.N.F., Jerusalem. Photo Malafsky, Jerusalem.

(mostly uncultivable land, e.g., the southern Negev), and 3,175,000 dunams abandoned by Arabs during the War of Independence.

Under a series of laws enacted in 1950 and 1951, the government lands were vested in the State of Israel and administered by the State Property Office; the abandoned lands were vested in the Custodian of Absentee Property, while their administration was handed over to the Land Development Authority; a third category, lands formerly owned by Germans and seized during World War II by the Custodian of Enemy Property, were handed over to the Administrator General. In 1955, the State Properties Division was set up to administer all lands owned or held by the state. Although this step did away with most of the duplication, there was still the question of the land owned by the J.N.F. By agreement with the J.N.F. and the Zionist Organization, a single Israel Lands Authority to administer both state and J.N.F. lands was set up in 1960 under the Israel Lands Law and the Israel Lands Authority Law, both passed in the same year. The former, which is one of Israel's basic constitutional laws, lays down the principle that state, Development Authority, and J.N.F. lands shall not be sold, with exceptions specified in the law itself. The Israel Lands Authority Council consists of seven government and six J.N.F. representatives, with the minister of agriculture as chairman. Between May 1948 and June 1967 the J.N.F. acquired about 1,500,000 dunams from the Development Authority and a further few thousand dunams from Arabs. PICA transferred most of its holdings to the farmers in its villages and some 120,000 dunams to the J.N.F. At the beginning of 1968, the state and the Development Authority owned 16,200,000 dunams and the J.N.F., 2,570,000—making up 92% of the country's area. The Muslim waqf and Christian churches held 150,000 dunams and private persons (Jews and Arabs), 1,385,000.

10 LAND RECLAMATION

The Bible describes the reclamation of hilly terrain as practiced in the Land of Israel in ancient times. The viticulturist in the hills of Judea prepared his plot by digging and clearing stones before planting his vines (Isa. 5:2). Clearing stones and terracing occupy an important place in the *halakhot* dealing with land in the Mishnah and Talmud. Dry-stone walls (in mishnaic terminology *gappot* (Pe'ah 6:2); in Arabic *sinsala*) prevented the rain from sweeping the soil away into the lowlands and enabled it to be absorbed where it fell. The hill regions remained fertile as long as the terraces remained intact, but when the country was overrun by Bedouin, the walls were neglected and collapsed, so that the soil was exposed to erosion. As the prophet foretold: "The mountains shall be thrown down, and the steep places (Heb. *madregot*—"steps," or "terraces") shall fall, and every wall shall fall to the ground" (Ezek. 38:20).

In the second half of the 19th century some of the ancient terraces were repaired and new ones built. With the start of Jewish settlement in the 1880s, all types of land reclamation were utilized: swamp drainage by planting eucalyptus trees in Petaḥ Tikvah and Ḥaderah, stone clearing, deep plowing and terracing for vineyards and orchards in Zikhron Ya'akov, Rosh Pinnah, and Moẓa. Under the British Mandate the Jewish National Fund sponsored the drainage of 87,000 acres (350,000 dunams) of swamps in the Jezreel, Zebulun, Ḥefer, and Ḥuleh valleys, and the reclamation of 4,000 acres (16,000 dunams) of hilly terrain. In the same period PICA reclaimed the Kabarah swamp and others totaling 37,500 acres (150,000 dunams), while 22,500 acres (90,000 dunams) were reclaimed by other agencies.

The greater part of the uncultivated area in Israel consists of the Judean and Negev deserts, which support only desert vegetation and cannot be utilized even after reclamation unless supplied with water. Most of the other categories may be reclaimed by mechanical means. Hard soil—stony or rocky—or steep terrains, unfit for cultivation even if the earth between the boulders or under the stony stratum is fertile or sustains useful wild plants, is common in hill regions, of which there are about 1,080,000 acres (4,242,000 dunams), apart from deserts. About 48% of this area is cultivable, but some 550,000 acres (2,200,000 dunams) can be utilized only after reclamation by stone clearing, deep plowing—including removal of boulders, embedded rock or outcrops (and terracing) and construction of stone revetments along the declivities to form terraces and prevent soil erosion. If the ground still harbors superfluous trees and shrubs, these have to be extirpated. Swampland, waterlogged for the whole or the greater part of the year, cannot be utilized for agriculture without draining. Scrub soil, choked with undesirable wild brush or

Clearing stones in a land reclamation project at Biranit in Upper Galilee, 1964. Courtesy J.N.F., Jerusalem.

grasses, requires deep plowing and root clearance. Saline soil, common in the Negev, the Arabah, and the Plain of Jericho, is ameliorated by leaching out the salts, which entails the use of 2,000–3,000 cu. m. of water per dunam. Gullied soil, where the earth has been swept away and eroded by flash floods due to unskilled plowing of the slopes, is common all over the country, in particular in the southern and northern Negev. It may be reclaimed by filling in the gullies, leveling, and channeling to divert flood-water runoff. Unstable or sandy soil, such as the coastal dunes or the loess of the western Negev, may be utilized for intensive irrigated farming after amelioration with green and organic fertilizers.

In the period preceding statehood (1904–47) the Jewish National Fund reclaimed 11,120 acres (45,395 dunams) of which 5,778 acres (23,550 dunams) are in the hills and 5,342 acres (21,845 dunams) in the lowlands. Between 1948 and 1971, the total rose to 119,293 acres (486,000 dunams) of which almost 90% are in the hill regions or in the Negev. Another 110,456 acres (450,000 dunams) have been won by the J.N.F. through drainage of swamps and agricultural drainage. The reclaimed land serves for intensive, mostly irrigated, farming of fruit orchards, vegetable gardens and field crops. Since the State-J.N.F. Agreement of 1960, the J.N.F., functioning as the Israel Land Development Authority, serves as the exclusive agent for all reclamation work, irrespective of ownership of the reclaimed land.

11 THE JEWISH NATIONAL FUND

The Jewish National Fund (Keren Kayemeth Leisrael) was founded on Dec. 29, 1901 at the Fifth Zionist Congress at Basle, which resolved: "The JNF shall be the eternal possession of the Jewish people. Its funds shall not be used except for the purchase of lands in Palestine and Syria."

The Hebrew name comes from the talmudic dictum on good deeds "the fruits of which a man enjoys in this world, while the capital abides *(ha-keren kayyemet)* for him in the world to come" (Pe'ah 1:1). A land fund was first suggested by Judah Alkalai in 1847. It was proposed by Hermann Schapira at the Katowice Conference in 1884 and again at the First Zionist Congress in 1897. Schapira based his idea of public ownership of land on the biblical injunction "The land shall not be sold forever for the land is Mine," and on the institution of the Jubilee Year, which stipulates that all holdings which have changed hands revert to their original owners in the 50th year (Lev. 25:10,23–24).

JNF leasehold contracts run for 49 years and can be prolonged by the lessee or his heirs as long as they serve the purpose specified; holdings may neither be united with other domains nor divided among several heirs; the lessee needs the lessor's consent if he wishes to use his holding for a purpose other than that stipulated in the contract; on rural tracts, the lessee must cultivate his own soil; ground rents are to be kept as low as possible, whether the land serves farming, industry, housing, or other purposes.

Early Activities. Between 1902 and 1907, the JNF had its administration in Vienna, where Johann Kremenezki created a worldwide organization for fund raising by means of JNF stamps, the Blue Box, a small tin collection box, and the Golden Book for honoring a person by donating a large contribution in his name which is inscribed in the book, which soon became popular Zionist symbols. In 1907 the head office was transferred to Cologne, with Max Bodenheimer as chairman of the board of directors, and the JNF was incorporated in London as an "association limited by guarantee." The first tract of land acquired was that of Kefar Ḥittim in Lower Galilee (1904), followed in 1908 by Ben Shemen and Ḥuldah in Judea, and Kinneret-Deganyah near Lake Kinneret. The JNF made its first experiments in tree planting in 1908 with the Herzl Forest, financed by its Olive Tree Fund. It aided urban development by long-term loans to the founders of Tel Aviv and by acquiring the building of the Bezalel Art School in Jerusalem, land for the Herzlia High School in Tel Aviv, and the Technion in Haifa. It also financed the activities of the Palestine Office of the Zionist Organization. In 1914, with the outbreak of World War I, the head office was transferred to the Hague in neutral Holland under Nehemia de Lieme. In July 1920, the London Conference of the Zionist Organization, which established an additional fund, the Keren Hayesod, declared the JNF to be "the instrument of the urban and rural land policy of the Jewish people," devoted exclusively to land acquisition and improvement.

Under the Mandate. The first large settlement area was acquired in 1921 in the Jezreel Valley ("The Emek"), increasing JNF land property from 4,000 to almost 15,000 acres (16,000 to 59,000 dunams) after a violent debate with Zionist leaders who preferred the acquisition of urban holdings. In 1922, the head office was transferred to Jerusalem, and Menahem Ussishkin became its president. During the later 1920s, it acquired the Emek Ḥefer, creating a continuous chain of Jewish settlement in the coastal plain, with the Plain of Zebulun as hinterland to Haifa port. The Arab riots of 1936–39, and the Peel Commission's partition plan (1937–38) lent increased political importance to JNF land acquisition. Holdings and "stockade and watchtower" settlements were rapidly extended to new regions

(Beth-Shean and Ḥuleh valleys, Manasseh Hills, Western Galilee, southern Coastal Plain). During World War II, the JNF sought intricate legal expedients to overcome the severe restrictions imposed in February 1940 by the land regulations issued under the British White Paper, and stepped up land acquisition even further. Opening up the northern Negev for Jewish settlement and strengthening positions in Galilee, it brought its possessions in 1947 to 234,000 acres (936,000 dunams), more than half the total Jewish holdings in Palestine. After Ussishkin's death in 1941, a committee of three—Berl Katzenelson, Rabbi Meir Bar-Ilan (Berlin), and Abraham Granott—headed the JNF board of directors. In 1945, Granott took over as chairman and on his death in 1960 was succeeded by Jacob Tsur.

In Independent Israel. With the founding of the State of Israel, the emphasis of JNF activity shifted from land purchase to land improvement and development as well as afforestation, headed by Joseph Weitz from the early 1920s. Besides swamp drainage (Jezreel Valley, Ḥefer and Zebulun plains, etc.), much was done for hill reclamation through stone clearing and terracing, principally along the 1949 armistice borders, opening new areas for settlement. In the Negev contour-line plowing, planting of shelter belts around fields, and leveling in of eroded terrain have won new areas for farming. The JNF's most important swamp-draining enterprise was that of the Ḥuleh Valley (1952–58). By 1967 the JNF had reclaimed a total of 120,000 acres (480,000 dunams) and another 125,000 acres (500,000 dunams) approximately through swamp draining, together totaling about a quarter of the 1.05 million acres of cultivated land inside Israel's 1966 borders. Up to 1947, the JNF planted 5,280,000 forest trees on approximately 5,000 acres. Annual planting equaled or exceeded these figures since 1948, bringing the total in 1967 to over 90,000,000 trees and 100,000 acres, in addition to thousands of acres of degenerated natural brush rehabilitated by adequate care.

 The JNF serves tourism by installing camping and picnic

grounds in its forests, and participates in landscaping national parks and nature reserves. As part of its reclamation and afforestation programs, it has paved over 1,200 miles (2,000 kilometers) of roads, particularly in border areas. It also constructs storage dams to make storm-flood water available for irrigation. The JNF has aided immigrant absorption by setting up "work villages" and providing work for newcomers, especially during periods of unemployment. Since the mid-1950s, the JNF has embarked on comprehensive regional development projects (the Adullam, Adoraim, Yatir regions in southern Judea, the Modi'in region in northern Judea, the Iron Hills and Mount Gilboa in Samaria, the Chorazim region north of Lake Kinneret, and, from 1963, Central Galilee bordering on Lebanon). In the 1960s, the JNF started building Naḥal outpost villages in reclaimed border areas.

In July, 1960, the Knesset passed a fundamental law on Israel land holdings, followed by the Israel Land Administration Law. An agreement between the JNF and the government, signed on August 1, 1960, set up an Israel Land Authority for the administration of all government and JNF holdings, with a council of seven government and six JNF representatives, and a Land Development Authority functioning in the JNF framework, with seven JNF and six government representatives on its council. The latter is responsible for land development and afforestation of all public land. In 1967, JNF land holdings totaled over 637,000 acres (2,549,000 dunams), including 332,500 acres (1,330,000 dunams) which the JNF acquired from the state after 1948. In 1967, the government approved a concession to the JNF for the development of state domain land totaling 125,000 acres (500,000 dunams).

The JNF derives its budget largely from contributions from world Jewry, which in the 1960s averaged IL24,000,000 per year; the balance of the IL56,000,000 budget comes from leasehold fees and other sources. It operates in approximately 40 countries. It engages in Zionist education in schools and youth movements both in

Israel and abroad; a JNF teachers' council is active in Israel, as well as in a number of Diaspora countries. The JNF is headed by a board of directors consisting of 26 members elected by the Zionist General Council and up to three governors nominated by the Zionist Executive.

12 PLANNING AND DEVELOPMENT

The National Plan. When independent Israel was founded (1948), the greater part of the population was concentrated in the coastal strip and the cities of Tel Aviv, Haifa, and Jerusalem. In view of the large influx of new immigrants and the need to settle the sparsely populated areas, the government adopted a policy for the balanced distribution of the population over the entire country. On the basis of this policy, a national plan was prepared for urban development by the building of new towns and rural development by the expansion of agriculture and the establishment of new villages.

The physical national plan envisaged a network of regional urban centers of various sizes—from small district towns, providing services for populations of 30,000–50,000, to towns serving 80,000–150,000 people each, as well as the big cities. Twenty-eight new towns were established in Israel's first two decades, mainly in the Negev and in western and northern Galilee.

The national plan for the balanced distribution of the population was revised from time to time. The 1950 plan provided for the needs of 2,650,000 people, while the 1954 scheme envisaged 2,500,000 in 1965. The plan was revised in 1958 for a population of 3,250,000; in 1965 for an expected population of 4,000,000 in 1982; in 1967 for 4,000,000; and in 1970 again for 5,000,000 at the end of the century. All these plans were based on the de facto borders delimited by the armistice agreements of 1949.

The plan not only laid down the siting of new urban centers and the expansion of existing towns, but also served as a guide for the alignment of roads and the location of industries, public institutions, national parks, and nature reserves. It comprised a map specifying regions of priority for directed development, which was designed to implement the balanced distribution policy. The country was divided into six regions, maximum financial and other incentives being offered for industrial and other enterprises established in regions of high priority.

The first step toward the preparation of the national plan for parks and nature reserves was a survey of antiquities, holy places and other historic sites, woodlands, and areas of zoological, geological, or geomorphic interest. One of the basic principles of national planning was to resist the encroachment of urban development on agricultural lands and to confine it, as far as possible, to non-fertile areas. Development projects were accordingly drawn up for the sand dunes along the coast in the vicinity of Caesarea, Netanyah, Ḥolon, Bat-Yam, Ashdod, and Ashkelon, and for the hills east of Haifa and Tel Aviv. Another fundamental principle was the preservation of the country's rich historic heritage and its characteristic landscape. Some new towns were built around existing ancient and medieval nuclei, such as Safed, Tiberias, Acre, Beth-Shean, Nazareth, and Ashkelon, special care being given to their historical centers.

The Plan for Jerusalem. The plan for Jerusalem, which covered the entire city, is of special interest. In keeping with the topography of the capital, which has profoundly influenced its character, the hilltops and mountain slopes were specified for building purposes, constituting compact neighborhood units, while the valleys were left open as public areas. Special attention was paid to holy places and archaeological sites, and typical quarters of special interest were preserved. The open spaces form a suitable setting for public buildings, mostly on the hilltops, such as the Knesset, the government offices, the University, Herzl's tomb, Yad Vashem (the memorial to the victims of the Nazi Holocaust), and the Hadassah Hospital. A special team of experts, set up by the Ministry of the Interior and the Municipality, prepared plans for areas of special historical and religious importance, including the Old City, the Mount of Olives, and their environs. Special attention was paid to the Old City and very strict regulations laid down to preserve its character.

Rural Planning. In 1948, the Jewish rural population of Israel numbered about 85,000 in 320 villages. Despite central initiative, most agricultural development had been sporadic and uncoordinated, with no comprehensive planning, though the *yishuv's* planners had considerable achievements to their credit in the detailed planning of individual kibbutzim and moshavim. It was only after the attainment of independence, when all arbitrary restrictions on Jewish settlement had been swept away, that comprehensive development was possible.

Agricultural development was now planned by the Israel government in cooperation with the Jewish Agency's Settlement Department, on the basis of a countrywide survey of soil properties and land classification, and was integrated with the systematic exploitation of water resources.

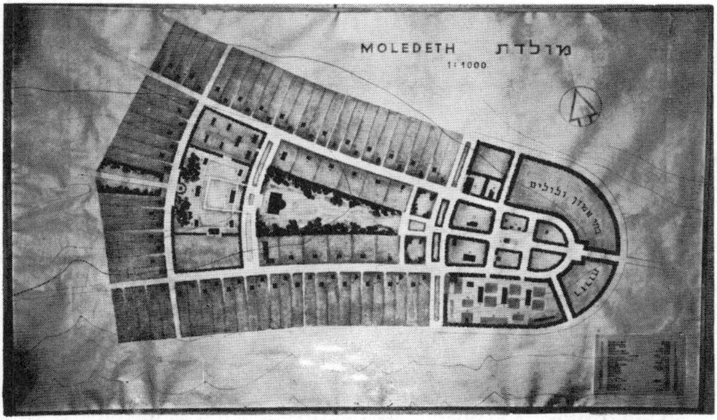

Plan of Moshav Moledet by Richard Kaufmann, 1947. Courtesy Keren Hayesod, United Israel Appeal, Jerusalem.

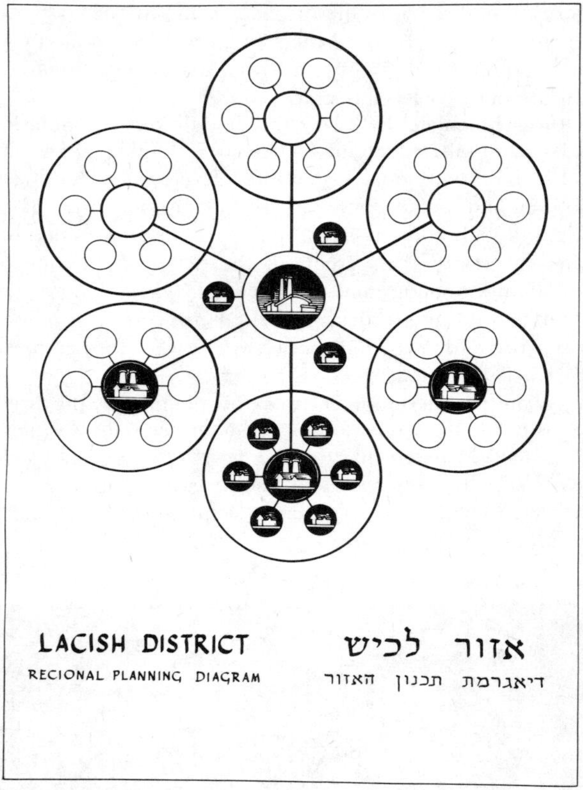

Lachish district planning diagram, showing clusters of moshavim around local centers radiating from the regional center, Kiryat Gat. Courtesy Jewish Agency Planning Department, Jerusalem.

Legislation. Planning procedures and activities are regulated by the Planning and Building Law, 1965, which is administered by the National Planning Board, six district planning commissions, special planning commissions, and local planning and building commissions. The main function of the National Board is to prepare national outline schemes, approve district outline schemes, and advise the government on all planning and building matters. There is a committee for the protection of agricultural land under the auspices of the National Board. The most important functions of the district planning commissions are to approve local outline schemes and detailed plans, and to draw up district outline schemes. The country is divided into town planning areas, each with a local planning and building commission, which prepares local planning schemes and detailed schemes, issues building permits, etc.

The Minister of the Interior may, upon the recommendation of the Minister of Housing, declare by order that any area situated within one district shall be a special planning area. Every such area has a special planning and building commission, which acts, with certain restrictions, as a local and district commission. Other provisions of the law deal with expropriation, compensation, defense installations and obstructions to aviation, non-conforming use, offenses, penalties, and miscellaneous matters. The Minister of the Interior is charged with the implementation of the law and may make regulations after consultation with the National Board.

13 HOUSING

To End of the Mandatory Period. Throughout the history of modern Palestine, the construction of housing by settlers played a dominant role in the country's economic life. Before World War I, and up to the early 1930s, industry and agriculture were not on a large enough scale to provide immediate employment for new immigrants, and building was the occupation in which they could be absorbed almost as soon as they stepped off the boat. In 1925 no less than 43% of all Jewish workers were employed in construction, and in 1926/27 the percentage was still 34.2. It was only in the 1930s, after the rapid development of industry and agriculture, that the share of construction in total employment was sharply reduced, declining to 19.4% in 1935 and 11% in 1936. Even so, construction remained an important factor in the economy, and in the period 1932–39 it accounted for as much as 47% of capital investment from Jewish sources.

JEWISH HOUSING QUARTERS. Even before the period of modern resettlement, Jews tended to leave the traditional confines of the old, established cities in order to establish their own urban quarters. As early as 1860, a group of Jewish inhabitants left the unsanitary and overcrowded Old City of Jerusalem and took the revolutionary step of moving into a new quarter outside the city walls, Mishkenot Sha'ananim, founded by Moses Montefiore. Later, two other quarters were established: Naḥalat Shiv'ah (1869) and Me'ah She'arim (1873). This trend was continued by the new settlers who came to the towns. At first they found homes in Jaffa, Jerusalem, or another of the existing cities, but after a while they sought to establish more modern and

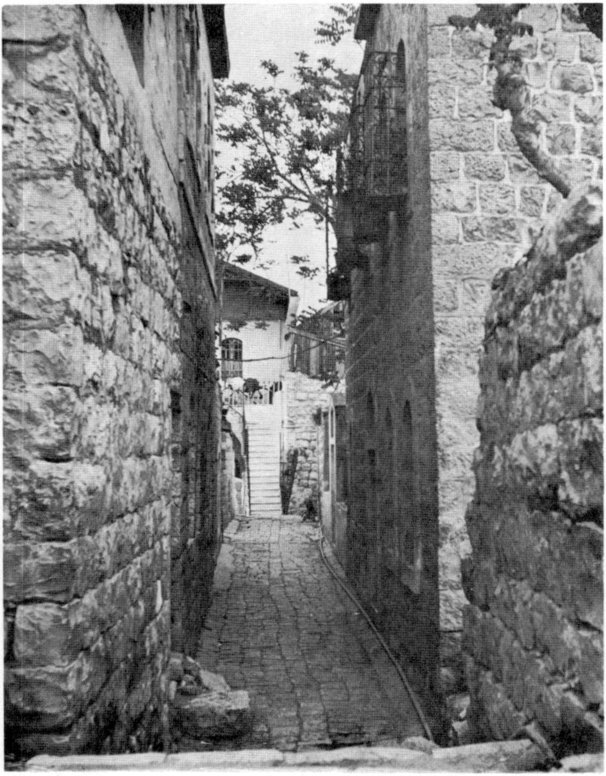

Alleyway in Naḥalat Shiv'ah, Jerusalem, 1955. The quarter was founded in 1869. Courtesy Jewish Agency, Jerusalem.

spacious quarters for themselves. Perhaps the most striking example was the founding in 1909 (by a group of Jaffa Jews) of Tel Aviv, which, from a mere suburb, became the country's largest city. New Jewish quarters were also founded in Jerusalem (Beit ha-Kerem, Talpiyyot, Reḥavyah, Kerem Avraham) and Haifa (Hadar ha-Karmel, Har ha-Karmel, Kiryat Ḥayyim, Kiryat Motzkin, etc.). A variety of factors contributed to this trend. In addition to the desire to escape from the primitive conditions of the Arab urban centers, there was the urge to create completely Jewish surroundings; to live among people of the same origin and background, or among equally observant Jews; and to enhance security. Furthermore, the price of land inside the old cities was too high to permit the construction of popular housing on any appreciable scale.

EXPANSION OF BUILDING. Every new wave of immigration resulted in an expansion of building activity. In 1934–35, the record year for immigration in the Mandatory period, housing construction reached unprecedented heights, while at the end of the 1930s, when immigration was curtailed, there was a corresponding decline in building. As a rule, however, the rate of construction lagged behind demand and severe housing shortages arose. A census taken in 1937 disclosed that 40% of Histadrut members had less than one room to accomodate their families, while only 15% lived in two-room apartments. The price of land soon became a severe problem in the new Jewish cities and quarters. This brought about a sharp rise in the cost of rented dwellings, which, it became apparent, could not solve the housing problem. On the eve of World War II the price of a building plot accounted for 30–50% of the capital investment required for housing. Credit was another problem: the rate of interest was high (8–9%) and adequate mortgages were not available, so that the builder had to look for additional finances, which was even more expensive. During the war rents were frozen by law, while prices and building costs kept rising. The controlled rents no longer had any realistic relationship to actual building costs. The result was the introduction of "key money," a large one-time payment to the landlord and the former tenant whenever an apartment changed hands. For the lower-income groups, the war veterans and the refugees from Europe, this payment was too heavy a burden.

PUBLIC HOUSING. As a result of this situation, various forms of public and cooperative housing came to the fore.

This was not a new feature; most of the Jewish quarters and towns were founded by building societies. In the course of time, large housing companies were established and sought to lower the costs and lessen the burden upon the individual. They obtained low-cost land from the Jewish National Fund and mortgages from public or semi-public financial institutions on comparatively easy terms; lowered contractors' profits; and introduced more rational and standardized construction methods. The Histadrut Labor Federation played a leading role in this field since its early years by building workers' quarters (Shekhunat Borochov, near Tel Aviv, built in 1922, was the first) and in 1935 had founded its own housing company, Shikkun, which built houses for immigrants and, after World War II, for war veterans. In addition, the Histadrut founded Neveh Oved, a housing company for agricultural laborers, and Shikkun Amami, for non-Histadrut low-income groups. Another large housing company was Rassco (Rural and Suburban Settlement Co.), founded by the Jewish Agency, which had been engaged in the settlement of middle-class immigrants on the land and now went in for urban housing as well. Some of the political parties had their own housing companies, and in 1945 the municipalities were also authorized by the government to provide housing. The growing share of public and semi-public housing companies in residential construction after the war is illustrated by the figures for 1945–46, when they were responsible for the construction of 12,742 rooms out of 29,000 built for the Jewish population, or 44% of the total.

In the State of Israel. THE EARLY YEARS. Housing was one of the most pressing problems faced by the infant state. While the population doubled by immigration in the first three years of the State, improved housing for the existing population was urgently needed. At the end of 1949, the government established a Housing Division, which became the main agency for immigrant housing, as a branch of the Ministry of Labor and put at its disposal budgetary funds, land in various parts of the country, and the planning facilities of the Government Planning Division. The building-materials industry also adapted itself to the growing needs. Other important factors which facilitated the execution of a great housing program in these years were the training of building workers and the experience gained in earlier periods by public and private construction companies.

The rate of construction grew by leaps and bounds: from 843,000 sq. m. in 1949 to 2,137,000 in 1952. There was a slowdown in 1953, but the rate picked up again the following year and continued to be high for most of 1955. The number of building workers increased considerably, but not sufficiently to meet demand, and there was a scarcity of building materials; consequently, the quality of the houses built in this period was rather low. Housing and public works accounted for 45% of all capital invested in 1949, 44% in 1950, and 70% in 1951. Building on this scale was one of the principal causes of the inflation that marked the Israel economy in this period. The pressing needs forced

"Shikkun Alef" in Beersheba, one of the first housing projects for new immigrants, built in 1951. Courtesy Government Press Office, Tel Aviv.

the government to finance two-thirds of all construction, including practically all immigrant housing, public buildings, and housing for special groups. The government was able to use housing to effect a greater dispersal of the population, resulting in an increase in the percentage of the rural and semi-rural population. Private building, accounting for the remaining third, supplied the needs of the established residents.

A unique aspect of housing in Israel was the fact that only a small percentage was built for rental. This was partly due to the freezing of rents by the Tenants' Protection Law 1954, and although rents were raised from time to time, they did not provide sufficient incentive for investors. Moreover, due to the high cost of building, rentals had to be subsidized if they were not to be too high for the great majority of tenants. In view of the need for economy and the avoidance of inflation, therefore, the government favored apartment purchase wherever possible.

IMPROVED STANDARDS. As the standard of living rose, large sectors of the population sought to improve their accommodations. The average size of publicly built apartments grew from 44.6 sq. m. in 1955 to 77.4 sq. m. in 1968; in the latter year privately built apartments averaged 98.4 sq. m. The average number of rooms per apartment also grew: from 2.0 in 1955 to 2.9 in 1968. There was also a general improvement in the finish of the apartments, as well as planning and environmental services. The owner's share in the financing of construction grew appreciably and a considerable part of the finance was raised by stocks issued by financial institutions.

In 1955 a Saving-for-Housing Scheme was introduced by the government, designed to facilitate saving and the use of the proceeds to finance current construction. By the end of 1967, some 70,000 apartments had been built under this scheme, which from 1961 no longer received aid from the government development budget (except for houses built in development towns). Building was increasingly mechanized: modern equipment made it possible to accelerate the rate of construction and erect high-rise buildings (a matter of necessity in view of the increase in land prices after 1960, especially affecting private housing). Most of the public building in this period was for new immigrants. Almost half of immigrant housing was constructed in the new development towns, adding further to the dispersal of the population. In 1961 the Housing Division became a separate ministry. This has facilitated advances in the standard of housing and its planning and adaptation to the general development of the country and its social aims.

HOUSING FOR IMMIGRANTS. It was immigration that was responsible for the extraordinary dimensions of the housing problem in the State of Israel: in two decades homes had to be built for a trebled population, the newcomers carrying with them the habits and the prejudices of sharply contrasting cultures from East and West. The housing authorities had not only to provide them with a roof, but also to establish the conditions for immigrants from a hundred countries to live harmoniously together and adapt policies to the needs of a rapidly developing modern

Housing in Ashdod. The earlier, two-family units are in the foreground, and later, multi-family dwellings in the background. Courtesy Government Press Office, Tel Aviv.

Ramat Yosef, a residential area in Bat Yam, 1964. Courtesy Government Press Office, Tel Aviv.

economy. In the five years 1948–53, during which the population grew by 117%, homes had to be built rapidly with inadequate resources in money, materials, and skilled labor. Inevitably, improvised solutions had to be adopted. Abandoned Arab housing provided a breathing space, but thousands had to be accommodated in camps. The Housing Division of the Ministry of Labor cooperated with the Jewish Agency officials in choosing locations for 123 *ma'barot* all over the country and put up every kind of temporary shelter, using wood, corrugated iron, asbestos boards, and canvas stretched over wooden frames.

The next stage was the erection of permanent housing in the old and new villages, in the suburbs, and on the sites of *ma'barot*. Owing to the tremendous pressure, standards were necessarily low: houses were built of the cheapest materials by methods suitable for the relatively unskilled manpower available. The area of the dwellings ranged from 28 to 54 sq. m.; they were often handed over to the tenants barely finished, without internal doors to the rooms, except for lavatories and bathrooms, and the occupants had to make do with a shower until they could find the money to install a bath. It was only in the second half of the 1950s that some progress in housing standards was possible. In the 1960s, and especially with the growing immigration of Jews from Western countries, standards became, on the whole, reasonably satisfactory.

In the early stages, the immigrants themselves, though unskilled, were given employment in the building of their own homes, and as much use as possible was made of materials available in the neighborhood. The building industry became steadily mechanized. Thirteen plants for the manufacture of prefabricated structures were established, and a degree of mechanization was introduced in conventional building methods. From the establishment of the state until 1970, 40,000,000 sq. m. of housing have been built for the accommodation of immigrants and other social purposes. In addition to dwellings, the state also had to erect in the new villages, towns, and suburbs buildings for public services, such as commercial centers, industrial estates, schools and kindergartens, synagogues, cultural centers, and cinemas.

SLUMS AND OVERCROWDING. Slums and defective or inadequate housing were created by: (1) the rapid deterioration of abandoned Arab houses in some of the larger towns and the Jewish quarters constructed before World War I (some of these could be repaired, while others had to be pulled down and the inhabitants rehoused); (2) the building of small and overcrowded, though generally sound and habitable, apartments in the early years of the state (rooms were added where possible, two adjacent apartments turned into one, and large families transferred to more spacious quarters); (3) the continued occupancy of some temporary buildings by immigrants (these were gradually transferred to permanent homes and the buildings demolished). A Slum Clearance and Building Authority was set up under the Clearance and Building Law of 1965 to deal with the legal, social, economic, and planning aspects of the problem. Tasks still to be tackled were: reexamination of housing operations in the past, with a view to correcting planning and other defects of the work done in the early years of the state; more building in the development towns to provide accommodation for the growing population; and speeding up slum clearance.

From 1948 to 1967, 600,000 units of permanent housing were built in Israel, 225,000 by private enterprise and 375,000 by public bodies.

SINCE THE SIX-DAY WAR. The demand for housing rose steeply after the Six-Day War because of a rapid rise in incomes and living standards after two years of recession, increased immigration, and a higher marriage-rate. As it took time to put the building industry into high gear, the demand considerably outstripped the supply and prices rocketed, so that young couples found it harder to buy homes and poor families to improve their housing conditions. These difficulties led to much discontent and criticism, some of which was directed against the immediate provision of comparatively roomy housing for newcomers.

The Government took steps to get more houses built for young couples and slum-dwellers, while, at the same time, meeting the needs of the rising immigration. The allocation for investment in housing in the 1972/73 budget was IL869 million, compared with IL130 million in 1967/68, making it the third-highest item, after defense and education. Measures were also taken to modernize the industry by having more and more components made in the factory and reducing the amount of work to be done on the site.

The result was a steady increase in the number of houses started and completed, as shown in the accompanying table. The number of families living in conditions of overcrowding—three persons or more per room—fell from about 100,000 in the early sixties to 47,000 in 1971 and a five-year plan was adopted to do away with this degree of overcrowding by 1976. Financial and other arrangements were made to house 42,000 young couples—18,000 by the

Table 11. Residential Building, 1967–1971

Dwellings Started			
	Public Building	Private Building	Total
1967	9,230	9,750	18,980
1968	8,430	15,830	24,260
1969	13,520	23,420	36,940
1970	21,320	24,700	46,020
1971	17,880	33,050	50,930
Totals	70,380	106,750	177,130
Dwellings Completed			
	Public Building	Private Building	Total
1967	12,570	15,330	27,900
1968	9,440	13,160	22,600
1969	9,150	16,480	25,630
1970	11,160	20,180	31,340
1971	15,600	22,770	38,370
Totals	67,920	87,920	145,840

Source: Central Bureau of Statistics

government and the rest through public companies and large constructors—in 1972 and 1973 at less than market prices. It was expected that by the middle of the decade the backlog in this type of housing would be overcome, leaving the manageable problem of housing each year's newly married couples in their turn.

GLOSSARY

Aliyah, (1) immigration to Ereẓ Israel; (2) one of the waves of immigration to Ereẓ Israel from the early 1880s.

Amora (pl. **amoraim**), title given to the Jewish scholars in Ereẓ Israel and Babylonia in the third to sixth centuries who were responsible for the *Gemara.*

Betar, activist Zionist youth movement, founded in 1923, associated with the Revisionist and Herut movements.

Bet ha-midrash, school for higher rabbinic learning; often attached to or serving as synagogue.

Bilu, first modern movement for pioneering and agricultural settlement in Ereẓ Israel, founded in 1882 at Kharkov, Russia.

Dayyan, member of rabbinic court.

Diaspora, Jews living in the "dispersion" outside Ereẓ Israel; area of Jewish settlement outside Ereẓ Israel.

Dunam, unit of land area (1,000 sq. m., c. 1/4 acre), used in Israel.

Ereẓ Israel, Land of Israel; Palestine.

Exilarch, lay head of Jewish community in Babylonia.

Hadassah, the Women's Zionist Organization of America which undertakes health and welfare activities in Israel.

Haganah, clandestine Jewish organization for armed self-defense in Ereẓ Israel under the British Mandate, which eventually evolved into a people's militia and became the basis for the Israel army.

Hakhsharah ("preparation"), organized training in the Diaspora of pioneers for agricultural settlement in Ereẓ Israel.

Halakhah (pl. **halakhot**), an accepted decision in rabbinic law. Also refers to those parts of the Talmud concerned with legal matters.

Ḥalutz (pl. **ḥalutzim**), pioneer, especially in agriculture, in Ereẓ Israel.

Ha-Po'el ha Za'ir, labor Zionist party founded in Ereẓ Israel in 1905. It merged with Po'alei Ẓion and non-party elements in 1930 to form Mapam (Israel Labor Party).

Ḥasid (pl. **Ḥasidim**), adherent of Ḥasidism.

Ḥasidism, (1) religious revivalist movement of popular mysticism among Jews of Germany in the Middle Ages; (2) religious movement founded by Israel ben Eliezer Ba'al Shem Tov in the first half of the 18th century.

Haskalah, "Enlightenment"; movement for spreading modern European culture among Jews c. 1750–1880.

He-Halutz, an association of Jewish youth in Diaspora training its members to settle on the land in Israel.

Ḥibbat Zion, see Ḥovevei Zion.

Histadrut (abbr. for Heb. **Ha-Histadrut ha-Kelalit shel ha-Ovedim ha-Ivriyyim be-Ereẓ Israel**), Ereẓ Israel Jewish Labor Federation, founded in 1920; subsequently renamed Histadrut ha-Ovedim be-Ereẓ Israel.

Holocaust, the organized mass persecution and annihilation of European Jewry by the Nazis (1933–1945).

Ḥovevei Zion, federation of Ḥibbat Zion, early (pre-Herzl) Zionist movement in Russia.

Jewish Agency, international, nongovernment body, centered in Jerusalem, which is the executive and representative of the World Zionist Organization.

Jewish Legion, Jewish units in British army during World War I.

Kabbalah, the Jewish mystical tradition.

Kabbalist, student of Kabbalah.

Karaite, member of a Jewish sect originating in the eighth century which rejected rabbinic Judaism and accepted only Scripture as authoritative.

Kevuẓah, small commune of pioneers constituting an agricultural settlement in Ereẓ Israel (evolved later into kibbutz).

Kibbutz (pl. **kibbutzim**), larger-size commune constituting a settlement in Ereẓ Israel based mainly on agriculture but engaging also in industry.

Knesset, parliament of the State of Israel.

Kolel, (1) community in Ereẓ Israel of persons from a particular country or locality, often supported by their fellow countrymen in the Diaspora; (2) institution for higher Torah study.

Kuppat Holim, "sick fund", cooperative medical insurance fund; under the auspices of the Histadrut, the General Federation of Labor.

Ma'abarah, transition camp; temporary settlement for newcomers in Israel during the period of mass immigration following 1948.

 Mandate, Palestine, responsibility for the administration of

Palestine conferred on Britain by the League of Nations in 1922; mandatory government; the British administration of Palestine.

Minyan, group of ten male adult Jews, the minimum required for communal prayer.

Mishnah, earliest codification of Jewish Oral Law.

Mitzvah, biblical or rabbinic injunction; applied also to good or charitable deeds.

Moshav, smallholders' cooperation agricultural settlement in Israel.

Moshav shittufi ("collective moshav"), agricultural village in Israel whose members possess individual homesteads but where the agriculture and economy are conducted as a collective unit.

Musar movement, ethical movement developing in the latter part of the 19th century among Orthodox Jewish groups in Lithuania; founded by R. Israel Lipkin (Salanter).

Nagid (pl. **negidim**), title applied in Muslim (and some Christian) countries in the Middle Ages to a leader recognized by the state as head of the Jewish community.

Nahal, branch of the Israel Defense Forces training cadres for agricultural settlements.

Nasi (pl. **nesi'im**), talmudic term for president of the Sanhedrin, who was also the spiritual head and, later, political representative of the Jewish people; from second century a descendant of Hillel recognized by the Roman authorities as patriarch of the Jews. Now applied to the president of the State of Israel.

Negev, the southern, mostly arid, area of Israel.

Oleh (pl. **Olim**), immigrant to Ereẓ Israel.

Partition plan(s), proposals for dividing Ereẓ Israel into autonomous areas or separate states.

Perushim, disciples of Elijah ben Solomon Zalman, the gaon of Vilna, who arrived in Ereẓ Israel during the second half of the 18th century.

PICA (The Palestine Jewish Colonization Association), society for Jewish settlement in Palestine active between 1924 and 1957, established by Baron Edmond de Rothschild.

Po'alei Zion, Socialist Zionist movement. In Ereẓ Israel, it merged with non-party elements and then with Ha-Po'el ha-Ẓa'ir in 1930 to form Mapai (Israel Labor Party). In the Diaspora, it became the main element in the World Zionist Labor Movement.

Rosh yeshivaḥ, see yeshivah.

Sanhedrin, the assembly of ordained scholars which functioned both as a supreme court and as a legislature before 70 C.E.

Shabbatean, adherent of the pseudo-messiah Shabbetai Ẓevi (17th century).

Shali'aḥ (pl. **sheliḥim**), in Jewish law, messenger, agent; in modern times, an emissary from Ereẓ Israel to Jewish communities or organizations abroad for the purpose of fund-raising, organizing pioneer immigrants, education, etc.

Shephelah, southern part of the coastal plain of Ereẓ Israel.

Six-Day War, brief war in June 1967 when Israel reacted to Arab threats and blockade by defeating the Egyptian, Jordanian, and Syrian armies.

Stockade and watchtower, type of settlement established in Palestine between 1936 and 1947 in planned surprise operation to provide immediate security against Arab attacks.

Talmud, "teaching"; compendium of discussions on the Mishnah by generations of scholars and jurists in many academies over a period of several centuries. The Jerusalem (or Palestinian) Talmud mainly contained the discussions of the Palestinian sages. The Babylonian Talmud incorporates the parallel discussion in the Babylonian academies.

Tanna (pl. **tannaim**), rabbinic teacher of mishnaic period.

Tosafist, talmudic glossator, mainly French (12th–14th centuries), bringing additions to the commentary by Rashi.

Tosafot, glosses supplied by tosafist.

Uganda Scheme, plan suggested by the British government in 1903 to establish an autonomous Jewish settlement area in East Africa.

Ulpan, center for intensive study by adults, especially of Hebrew by newcomers to Israel.

Va'ad Le'ummi, national council of the Jewish community in Ereẓ Israel during the period of the British Mandate.

Waqf (Ar.), (1) a Muslim charitable pious foundation; (2) state lands and other property passed to the Muslim community for public welfare.

War of Independence, war of 1947–49 when the Jews of Israel fought off Arab invading armies and ensured the establishment of the new State.

White Paper(s), report(s) issued by British government, frequently statements of policy, as issued in connection with Palestine during the Mandate period.

Yeshivah, Jewish traditional academy devoted primarily to study of rabbinic literature; *rosh yeshivah,* head of the yeshivah.

Yishuv, settlement; more specifically, the Jewish community of Ereẓ Israel in the pre-State period. The pre-Zionist community is generally designated the "old yishuv" and the community evolving from 1880, the "new yishuv."

ABBREVIATIONS

Ber.	*Berakhot* (talmudic tractate)
I (or II) Chron.	Chronicles, books I and II (Bible)
Dan.	Daniel (Bible)
Deut.	Deuteronomy (Bible)
Eccles.	Ecclesiastes (Bible)
Er.	*Eruvin* (talmudic tractate)
Esth.	Esther (Bible)
Ex.	Exodus (Bible)
Ezek.	Ezekiel (Bible)
Ezra	Ezra (Bible)
Gen.	Genesis (Bible)
Gen. R.	*Genesis Rabbah* (Midrash)
Git.	*Gittin* (talmudic tractate)
Hab.	Habakkuk (Bible)
Hag.	*Hagigah* (talmudic tractate)
Haggai	Haggai (Bible)
Hos.	Hosea (Bible)
Ḥul.	*Hullin* (talmudic tractate)
Isa.	Isaiah (Bible)
Jer.	Jeremiah (Bible)
Job	Job (Bible)
Joel	Joel (Bible)
Josh.	Joshua (Bible)
Judg.	Judges (Bible)
Ket.	*Ketubbot* (talmudic tractate)
Kil.	*Kilayim* (talmudic tractate)
Lam.	Lamentations (Bible)
Lev.	Leviticus (Bible)
Mal.	Malachi (Bible)
Nah.	Nahum (Bible)
Neh.	Nehemiah (Bible)
Num.	Numbers (Bible)
Obad.	Obadiah (Bible)

Pe'ah	*Pe'ah* (talmudic tractate)
Pes.	*Pesaḥim* (talmudic tractate)
Prov.	Proverbs (Bible)
Ps.	Psalms (Bible)
Ruth	Ruth (Bible)
I and II Sam.	Samuel, books I and II (Bible)
Shab.	*Shabbat* (talmudic tractate)
Sif. Deut.	*Sifrei Deuteronomy*
Song	Song of Songs (Bible)
Suk.	*Sukkah* (talmudic tractate)
TJ	Jerusalem Talmud or Talmud Yerushalmi
Zech.	Zechariah (Bible)
Zeph.	Zephaniah (Bible)
Zev.	*Zevaḥim* (talmudic tractate)

BIBLIOGRAPHY

Aliyah: Seminar ha-Kibbutzim, *Ha-Aliyah ha-Rishonah, Goremeha ha-Ra'yoniyyim ve-ha-Re'aliyyim* (1963); B. Habas, *Sefer ha-Aliyyah ha-Sheniyyah* (1947); D. Giladi, *Ha-Yishuv bi-Tekufat ha-Aliyyah ha-Revi'it, 1924–1929* (1968), incl. bibl.; M. Basok, *Sefer ha-Ma'pilim* (1947); H. M. Sachar, *Aliyah . . .* (Eng., 1961); J. B. Schechtman, *On Wings of Eagles* (1961); S. Barer, *The Magic Carpet* (1957); idem, *From the Ends of the Earth* (1964); M. Sikron, *Immigration to Israel 1948–1953* (1957).

"Illegal" Immigration: M. M. Mardor, *Strictly Illegal* (1964); J. and D. Kimche, *Secret Roads* (1954); B. Habas, *Ha-Sefinah she-Nizzeḥah* (1948); idem, *Gate Breakers* (1963); M. Basok (ed.), *Sefer ha-Ma'pilim* (1947); H. Lazar, *Af Al Pi* (Heb., 1957); Dinur, Haganah, 2 pt. 3 (1964²), index s.v. *Ha'palah;* D. Niv, *Ma'arekhot ha-Irgun ha-Ẓeva'i ha-Le'ummi,* 2 (1965), 129–63; 3 (1967), 67–71, 321–34; J. Derogy, *La loi du retour; la secrète et véritable histoire de l'Exodus* (1968).

The Beriḥah: Y. Bauer, *Flight and Rescue* (1970); J. and D. Kimche, *The Secret Roads* (1954); *"Brycha" 1945–1948* (Pol., 1950?), an album; E. Dekel, *Bi-Netivei ha-"Berihah"* (1958); idem, in: *Seridei Ḥerev* (1963); A. Gefen, *Unholy Alliance* (1973); L. W. Schwarz, *The Redeemers* (1953), 232–45; R. Korchak, *Lehavot ba-Efer* (1965), 303–7.

Absorption: S. Sitton, *Israël, immigration et croissance 1948–1958 . . . (1963);* H. Isaacs, *American Jews in Israel* (1967); S. N. Eisenstadt et al. (eds.), *Integration and Development in Israel* (1970), incl. bibl.

Law of Return: S. Rosenne, in: *Journal du Droit international, 81(Eng., 1954), 5–63.*

Youth Aliyah: R. Freier, *Let the Children Come* (1961); C. Pincus, *Come from the Four Winds—The Story of Youth Aliyah* (1970); M. Kol, *Youth Aliyah—Past, Present and Future* (1957); idem, *Massekhel Aliyyat ha-No'ar* (1961); N. Bentwich, *Jewish*

Youth Comes Home (1944); Ch. Rinott, *No'ar Boneh Beito* (1953); idem, *Kavvim le-Aliyyat ha-No'ar ki-Tenu'ah Hinnukhit* (1951); idem, in: K. Frankenstein (ed.), *Between Past and Future* (1953).

Settlement: A. Bein, *The Return to the Soil, A History of Jewish Settlement in Israel* (1952) incl. bibl.; A. Ruppin, *The Agricultural Colonization of the Zionist Organization in Palestine* (1926); J. Ben David (ed.), *Agricultural Planning and Village Community* (UNESCO, *Arid Zone Research*, 23 (1964); R. Weitz and A. Rokach, *Agricultural Development: Planning and Implementation* (1968); R. Weitz, *Darkenu ba-Hakla'ut u-va-Hityashevut* (1958).

Land Ownership: J. Weitz, *Struggle for the Land* (1950); idem, *Bi-Netivai le-Yishuvah shel ha-Areẓ* (1960); A. Granott, *Land System in Palestine* (1952); idem, *Agrarian Reform and the Record of Israel* (1956); A. Bonné, *State and Economics in the Middle East* (1948).

Land Reclamation: J. Weitz, *Mi-Gamdah le Ravḥah.* From Desolation to Cultivation, a history of land reclamation in Israel (1972); E. Orni, D. H. Yaalon, *Reclamation and Conservation of the Soil* (1970^3).

Jewish National Fund: A. Boehm and A. Pollak, *Jewish National Fund* (1939); A. Granott, *Agrarian Reform and the Record of Israel* (1956); J. Tsur, *Old Concepts and New Realities* (1962); J. Weitz, *Activities and Tasks of the Jewish National Fund* (1933); idem, *Afforestation Policy in Israel* (1950); idem, *Struggle for the Land* (1950); *Reports of Keren Kayemeth Leisrael to the Zionist Congresses,* beginning from the Sixth Congress (1903–).

Planning: J. Dash and E. Efrat, *The Israel Physical Master Plan* (1964); A. Sharon, *Physical Planning in Israel* (1952); E. Brutzkus, *Physical Planning in Israel* (1964); E. Spiegel, *New Towns in Israel* (1967); J. Shuval, *Immigrants on the Threshold* (1963); A. Glikson, *Regional Planning and Development* (1955); M. D. Gouldman, *Legal Aspects of Town Planning in Israel* (1966); First World Congress of Engineers and Architects in Israel 1967, lecture by J. Dash; R. Weitz, *Ha-Kefar ha-Yisre'eli be-Iddan ha-Tekhnologyah* (1967); International Federation for Housing and Planning, *Proceedings of the 27th World Congress for Housing and Planning* (1964).

INDEX

Abiathar, 5
Abraham Dov of Ovruch, 11
Abraham Gershon of Kutow, 10
Abraham of Kalisz, 10
Abulafia, Ḥayyim, 10
Aden, 55
Aḥa of Shabḥa, 5
Algeria, 62
Al-Ḥarizi, Judah, 6
Aliyah Bet, *see* "Illegal" immigration
Aliyah Movement, 67-69
Alkalai, Judah, 112
Alliance Israélite Universelle, 17
American Jewish Joint Distribution Committee, 39,41,81
Amidar, 56
Amoraim, 4-5
Anan ben David, 5
Anglo-American Committee, 43, 47
Anglo-Palestine Company, 19
Arabs, 16, 23, 30, 33-34, 89 92-93, 106, 108, 113
Argentina, 69
Argov, Levi, *see* Kopelevich, Levi
Artzi, Yizhak, 81
Ashkenazi, Bezalel, 9
Australia, 66
Austria, 32, 39, 40, 42, 43, 48, 51, 73, 80, 112
Avigur, Shaul, 35, 40, 42

Ba'al Shem Tov, Israel, 10
Babylonia, 1, 4, 5
Baḥad, 21
Bak, Israel, 11
Bar-Ilan, Meir, 114
Basle Program, 75
Ben-Gurion, David, 20, 75
Benjamin of Tudela, 6
Ben-Nathan, Asher, 40
Ben-Ẓvi, Isser, 39
Ben-Ẓvi, Izhak, 20
Beriḥah, 37-43
Bernstein, Philip S., 41, 42
Bertinoro, Obadiah, 8
Betar, 21
Beyth, Hans, 80
Bilu, 14
Bodenheimer, Max, 113
Bordjel, Nathan, 10
Borochov, Ber, 17
Brazil, 69
Bukhara, 73
Bulgaria, 52

Burial, 2
Bussel, Yosef, 89

Canada, 66
Churchill, Winston, 23
Commandments, *see Mitzvot*
Constantine I, 5
Crusaders, 6, 7
Cukierman, Itzhak, 38, 41
Cyprus, 45, 46, 51, 81
Cyrus, 1
Czechoslovakia, 40, 41, 80

Daniel ben Azariah, 6
Daniel ben Moses al-Qūmisi, 5
Declaration of Independence, 50, 75
Dekel, Ephraim, 42, 43
De Lieme, Nehemia, 113
Displaced Persons, 38-43, 48, 51, 52

Education, 63, 70, 80-86, 115
Egypt, 61
Elazari-Volcani, Y.A., 89, 92
Eleazar ben Pedat, 4
Elijah of Ferrara, 7
England, 6, 22, 23, 29, 30, 33-36, 39, 44-47, 55, 66, 69, 80, 106
Estori ha-Parḥi, 7
Evian conference, 33
Exodus, 43, 46

France, 6, 7, 43, 46, 62, 66, 69
Frank, Ephraim, 40
Freier, Recha, 79

Georgia, 73
Germany, 7, 12, 30-33, 39-42, 46, 48, 51, 79, 80, 92
"Grabski Aliyah", 27
Granott, Abraham, 114

Haavara, 32
Ḥabad, 11
Hadassah, 32, 80, 85
Haganah, 26, 35, 36, 43, 44, 46
Haifa, 117, 123
Haimovich, Issachar, 40
Hananel ha-Bavli, 4
Hanan ha-Miẓri, 4
Ḥanina bar Ḥama, 4
Ha-Po'el ha-Ẓa'ir, 17
Harrison, Earl G., 40
Ḥasid, Judah, 9
Ḥasidism, 3, 10, 11, 66
Ḥayyim ben Attar, 10
Ḥayyim Greenberg Institute, 63
Ḥayyun, Gedaliah, 10
Hebrew National Liberation Committee, 44
He-Ḥalutz, 18, 20, 21, 26, 35
Herzl, Theodor, 16, 17
Ḥibbat Zion, 2, 14-16
Hillel, 4
Histadrut, 21, 25, 28, 79, 124-5

Ḥiyya ben Joseph, 5
Ḥiyya the Great, 4
Holland, 12
Horowitz, Isaiah ha-Levi, 9
Housing, 56, 57, 121-32
Ḥovevei Zion, *see* Ḥibbat Zion
Hungary, 12, 13, 41, 43, 61

ICA, *see* Jewish Colonization Association
"Illegal" immigration, 29, 34-36, 40, 43-45, 51
International Federation of Children's Communities, 86
International Union for Child Welfare, 86
Iraq, 52, 55, 56
Irgun Ẓeva'i Le'ummi, 43
Israel Land Development Authority, 111, 115
Israel of Shklov, 11
Israel Prize, 81
Issi ben Judah, 4
Italy, 7, 8, 51

Jehiel ben Joseph of Paris, 7
Jerusalem, 117-9, 122-3
Jewish Agency, 27-29, 31, 33, 35, 39, 50-52, 55-56, 59-62, 65-70, 80, 85, 92, 94, 119, 125, 129
Jewish Brigade, 39, 41, 81
Jewish Colonization Association, 88
Jewish National Fund, 19, 21, 22, 58, 89, 91, 106, 108, 109, 111-16, 125
Joffe, Eliezer, 91
Johanan ha-Sandelar, 4
Joseph da Montagna, 7
Judah Halevi, 6
Juedische Jugendhilfe, 79

Kahana, 5
Karaites, 2, 5, 9
Katowice Conference, 15, 112
Katzenelson, Berl, 114
Keren Hayesod, 22, 113
Keren Kayemet Leisrael, *see* Jewish National Fund
Kibbutz, 57, 59, 62, 66, 67, 79-81, 84, 90, 92, 98, 100
Kishinev pogroms, 17
Klarman, Yosef, 81
Kol, Moshe, 81
Kopelevich, Levi, 39
Kovner, Abba, 38
Kremenezki, Johann, 112

Landauer, Georg, 80
Latif, Isaac ben Meir, 7

Latin America, 65, 66
Law of Return, 50, 75, 76
Leningrad Trial, 72
Libya, 52
Loḥamei Ḥerut Israel, 43
London Conference, 22, 113
Luria, Shemariah, 11
Luzzatto, Moses Ḥayyim, 10

Ma'barah, 57-62, 129
Maimon ben Joseph, 6
Maimonides, 1, 7
Malakh, Ḥayyim, 9
Malki, Raphael Mordecai, 3
Mandate for Palestine, 23, 29, 30-49, 75, 106, 113-14, 124
Martin V, 7
Masaryk, Jan, 41
Menahem the Gaul, 4
Menahem Mendel of Peremyshlyany, 10
Menahem Mendel of Shklov, 11
Menahem Mendel of Vitebsk, 3, 10
Messianic Movements, 3
Mitzvot, 1, 2
Montefiore, Sir Moses, 106, 122
Morocco, 61
Moshav, 57, 59, 88, 89, 91, 92, 98, 99

Naḥmanides, 1, 7
Naḥman of Horodenko, 10
Nathan ha-Bavli, 4
New Zealand, 66

Oliphant, Laurence, 14
Operation Ezra and Nehemiah, 52, 55, 56
Operation Magic Carpet, 52, 55
O.S.E., 81

Palestine Jewish Colonization Association, 106, 108, 109
Palestine Office, 22, 24, 29, 89, 90, 113
Passfield, Lord, 30
Peel Commission, 31, 33, 113
Persia, 80
Perushim, 11
Pethahiah of Regensburg, 6
PICA, *see* Palestine Jewish Colonization Association
Pines, Yehiel, 14
Po'alei Zion, 17
Poland, 27, 38-42, 48, 52, 61, 73, 74, 80

Rabbi Ze'ev Gold Institute, 63
Rashish, Pinḥas, 39
Rassco, 125
Red Cross, 38, 40
Revisionists, 29, 35, 43, 44
Rifkind, Simon H., 41
Rivlin, Hillel, 11
Rokeaḥ, Eleazar, 10

Roosevelt, Eleanor, 86
Roosevelt, Franklin D., 33
Rothschild, Edmond de, 14, 16, 17, 87, 88
Rovigo, Abraham, 9
Rumania, 18, 38, 41, 43, 46, 52, 62
Ruppin, Arthur, 19, 89
Russia, 17-21, 26, 42, 48, 64, 70-73

Sacks, Moses, 12
Sahl ben Maẓli'aḥ, 5
Saladin, 6
Salant, Joseph Sundel, 11
Salant, Samuel, 11
Salmon ben Jeroḥam, 5
Sanhedrin, 7
Sapir, Meir, 43
Schapira, Hermann, 112
Schwarz, Jehoseph, 12
Sha'ar ha-Aliyah, 56
Shabbateanism, 9
Shalit Case, 77, 78
Sharabi, Shalom, 10
Shem Tov ben Abraham Gaon, 7
Sherut la-Am, 67
Shikkun, 125
Shikkun Amami, 125
Shlomel, Solomon, 2
Sholal, Isaac, 8
Six-Day War, 66, 70
Socialism, 17
Solomon ben Judah, 5
South Africa, 66, 69
Spain, 7, 8
Stockade and Watchtower, 92, 113
Surkis, Mordechai, 39
Swamps, 109, 114
Syria, 80, 112
Syrkin, Naḥman, 17
Szold, Henrietta, 32, 80

Ṭābū, 103
Tannaim, 4
Taxation, 103
Tel Aviv, 117, 123, 125
"Thousand Family Project", 92
Tiomkin, Vladimir, 16
Truman, Harry, 43, 47
Trumpeldor, Joseph, 18, 21
Tsur, Jacob, 114
Tunisia, 61
Turkey, 14, 103-6

Ulpan, 57, 62, 67, 85
United States of America, 27, 36, 40-43, 46, 66, 69
UNRRA, 40, 41
Ussishkin, Menahem, 113

Va'ad Le'ummi, 29
Vitkin, Joseph, 19

War of Independence, 93
War Refugee Board, 37
Weitz, Joseph, 114
Weizmann, Chaim, 30, 31
White Papers, 23, 24, 30, 33, 34, 46, 93, 114

World Zionist
Organization, 16, 21, 22, 50, 51

Yemen, 7, 8, 52, 55
Yeshivot, 2
Yoredim, 27
Yose ben Dormaskos, 4

Youth Aliyah, 32, 57, 63, 79-86

Zakkai, 4
Zionism, 16-38, 42, 89-92, 115
Zutra, Mar, 5